Learn to Crochet: A Beginner's Guide is Bendy Carter's 20th crochet pattern book for Annie's Attic. In the past she has written over 1,000 patterns which have been published in various magazines, books, leaflets and yarn company promotions.

Bendy learned to crochet around age 10. Her great aunt Beatrice taught her how to single crochet with thread while on vacation in Nebraska, but no mention of pattern books was made during their 1-hour meeting. Being so young, Bendy didn't know they existed. Bendy's dad purchased pink thread and a little crochet hook and she began "designing" her first baby doll blanket on the 2-day trip back home to Texas. Four years later she discovered pattern books, but many years passed before she got up the courage to send in one of her own designs for publication. The publisher not only accepted the design but requested more, and Bendy has been designing professionally ever since.

Bendy's favorite part of designing is creating new and interesting stitches. She says, "The idea that one can use a little stick with a hook on the end to turn a simple piece of string into anything imaginable still inspires me."

Although Bendy typically designs with yarn for publication, her hobby is still playing with thread to make tiny clothes for dollhouse dolls. If not playing with string, you will probably find her and her husband enjoying a peaceful evening in their small Texas town playing with their fur babies.

Table of Contents

2 Introduction

Part One
- 4 How to Start a Crochet Project
- 5 Chain Stitch (abbreviated ch or chs)
- 6 How to Finish a Crochet Project
- 6 Finished Measurements
- 7 **Chains of Love Heart**

Part Two
- 9 Tension on Foundation Chains
- 9 Single Crochet (abbreviated sc)
- 11 Help for Left-Handers
- 12 **Pretty Bow**

Part Three
- 14 How to Skip a Stitch
- 14 How to Make a Single Crochet Stitch in a Chain Space
- 14 What Is Gauge?
- 14 How to Add Fringe
- 15 **Woven Coaster**
- 17 **Washcloth Pals**

Part Four
- 19 Hanks of Yarn
- 19 Sewing
- 20 Single Crochet in Both Loops, Front Loop or Back Loop
- 20 Decorative Little Loop Edging
- 21 **Woolly Warmers**

Part Five
- 25 Pattern Information & Abbreviations
- 25 How to Join a New Color on a Row
- 25 How to Decrease at the Beginning of a Row
- 25 How to Whipstitch Pieces on Top of Pieces
- 26 **Mini Monster Pouch**

Part Six
- 31 Other Stitches
- 32 How to Increase
- 33 **Mystical Halves Scarf**

Part Seven
- 37 Double Crochet (abbreviated dc)
- 39 How to Change Color in the Last Two Loops of a Stitch
- 40 **Twisted Knot Ear Cozy**
- 42 **BONUS PROJECT: Twisted Knot Ear Cozy: Two Colors**

Part Eight
- 44 How to Join a Chain to Form a Ring
- 45 How to Crochet in a Ring
- 46 How to Find the End of a Round
- 46 How to End a Round With an Invisible Join
- 47 How to Join a New Color on a Round
- 48 **Pompom Tips Cap**
- 50 **BONUS PROJECT: Ye Olde Owl Cap**

Part Nine
- 54 How to Crochet in the Round Using Both Sides of a Chain
- 54 How to Crochet Two Pieces Together
- 55 **Window Panes Bag**

This book comes with step-by-step videos! Scan this code with your smartphone camera to access your videos.

Published by Annie's, 306 East Parr Road, Berne, IN 46711. Printed in USA. Copyright © 2025 Annie's. All rights reserved. This publication may not be reproduced in part or in whole without written permission from the publisher.

RETAIL STORES: If you would like to carry this publication or any other Annie's publication, visit AnniesWSL.com.

Every effort has been made to ensure that the instructions in this publication are complete and accurate. We cannot, however, take responsibility for human error, typographical mistakes or variations in individual work. Please visit AnniesCustomerService.com to check for pattern updates.

Welcome to the world of crochet!

Because learning a new craft can be a little intimidating for some, this book has been written in such a way that everyone can dive right into the art of crocheting with minimal up-front knowledge.

Before each pattern, you will find the crochet information needed to complete the project that follows. If this is your first experience with crochet, it will be helpful to work the projects in the order presented in the book as the knowledge required builds with each project.

To save print space, crochet patterns typically use a lot of abbreviations which many people find confusing when they are first starting. To keep things as simple as possible, no abbreviations will need to be learned to complete the projects in this book.

However, for those anxious "A+" students who would like to learn the common lingo used in crochet patterns, abbreviations will be added in parentheses following each word starting about halfway through the book.

For example, a sentence such as:
Single crochet in the next chain.
Will be written as:
Single crochet (sc) in the next chain (ch).

INTRODUCTION

Crochet, a French word meaning "hook," is a fun yarn craft for people of all ages.

To get started, you will only need seven items, most of which you probably already have:

1. Hook.
2. Yarn.
3. Tapestry needle.
4. Scissors.
5. Tape measure.
6. Locking stitch markers.
7. Project bag.

A few designs in this book will require embellishments such as wire, buttons, etc. Those will be listed, when needed, in the pattern.

HOOK:

There are many sizes and brands of hooks available. In this book, the patterns only call for:

A 5mm crochet hook (also known as H/8/5mm).

In case you need a larger or smaller hook to make your project the desired size, you might want to also have two additional hooks in your collection:

A 4mm crochet hook (also known as G/6/4mm).

A 5.5mm crochet hook (also known as I/9/5.5mm).

Try different brands of hooks out by holding them in your hand as if you were using them. Pick the brand that is most comfortable for you.

HOLDING THE HOOK:

There are many ways to hold a hook when using it. The two most common are shown below:

Knife hold.

Pencil hold.

YARN:

Choose a skein of worsted-weight, also called a #4 weight, smooth, light-colored yarn. Once you are confident in your abilities, any size or color of yarn, string or novelty fur can be chosen for future projects.

TAPESTRY NEEDLE:

Also known as a yarn needle. Choose one with a large enough eye to insert your yarn through.

TAPE MEASURE:

Any tape measure can be used— a retractable one is always fun but a plain school ruler can also be used for measuring. Something else to keep in mind is that plastic or fabric tape measures can stretch out over time. Replace them from time to time or stick with a good wood or metal ruler or tape measure.

PROJECT BAG:

Anything that will keep your tools and project together in one place will do, even a grocery bag or box, but of course, if budget allows, a pretty bag with lots of zipper pockets is always fun to have.

There is a lot more that could be said about each of these items and the other topics in this book. In an effort not to overwhelm you, we are keeping things simple and concise. As your crochet skills advance, you can research more on each item.

SCISSORS:

Scissors you already have will work, but if purchasing, a pair of folding scissors or scissors with protective closed tips work great as they are less likely to accidently cut your yarn when in your project bag.

LOCKING STITCH MARKERS:

Stitch markers come in a variety of shapes, colors, sizes and materials. Some stitch markers can be opened, while others cannot. For crochet projects, choose only stitch markers that can be opened and locked shut. You will need at least two different colors of markers.

Part One

HOW TO START A CROCHET PROJECT

There are at least two different ways to get the first loop of a project on your hook: making a twisted loop or slip knot *(loop)*.

Method 1. Leaving a 5-inch strand of yarn at the beginning, you can twist your hook around the yarn, creating a loop on your hook.

Or you can grab the yarn and give it a twist and set the loop on the hook. Then, pinch the base of it to hold it in place until you create the first stitch.

Method 2. Leaving a 5-inch strand of yarn at the beginning, loop the yarn as shown *(Fig. 1)*.

Insert the hook through the center of the loop and hook the free end *(Fig. 2)*.

Pull this through and up onto the working area of the hook *(Fig. 3)*.

Pull the free yarn end to tighten the loop *(Fig. 4)*.

It should be firm, but loose enough to slide back and forth easily on the hook. Be sure you still have about a 5-inch yarn end.

Hold the hook, now with its slip knot, in your dominant hand in your preferred grip.

Once you have that first twisted loop or knotted loop on your hook you can begin making chain stitches.

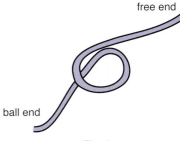

free end
ball end
Fig. 1

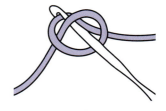

Fig. 2

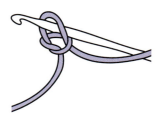

Fig. 3

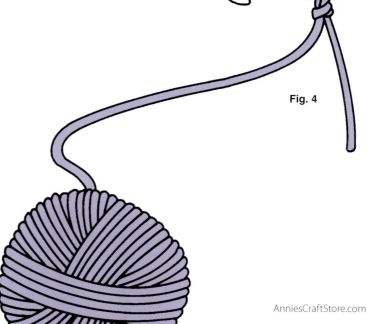

Fig. 4

CHAIN STITCH (ABBREVIATED CH OR CHS)

***NOTE:** Instructions are given for right-handed crocheters. Left-handers will work the opposite. For special help for left-handed crocheters, see page 11.*

Crochet usually begins with a series of chain stitches called a beginning or foundation chain.

Now, let's make the first chain stitch.

Step 1: Hold the base of the starting loop with the thumb and middle or index finger of your left hand; thread yarn from the skein over the middle or index finger *(Fig. 6)* and under the remaining fingers of your left hand *(Fig. 7)*.

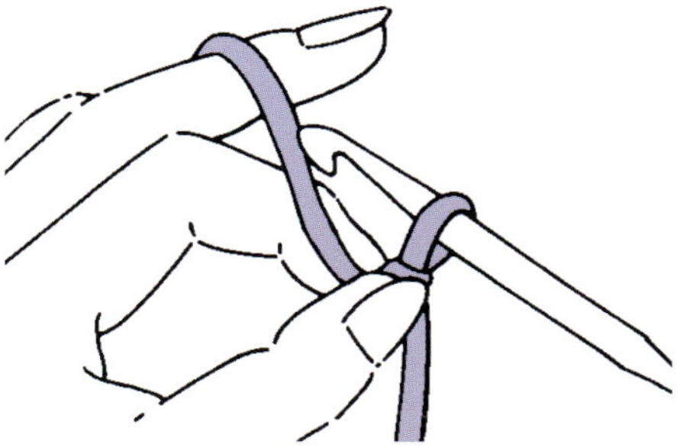

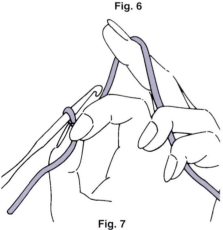

Fig. 6

Fig. 7

Your middle finger will stick up a bit to help the yarn feed smoothly from the skein; the other fingers help maintain even tension on the yarn as you work.

***HINT:** As you practice, you can adjust the way your left hand holds the yarn to however it is most comfortable for you.*

Step 2: Bring the yarn over the hook from back to front and hook it *(Fig. 8)*.

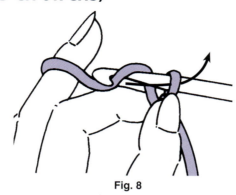

Fig. 8

Draw hooked yarn through the loop of the slip knot on the hook and up onto the working area of the hook *(see arrow on Fig. 8)*; you have now made one chain stitch *(Fig. 9)*.

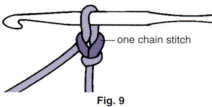

Fig. 9

Step 3: Again, bring the yarn over the hook from back to front *(Fig. 10)*.

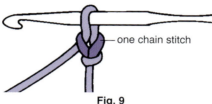

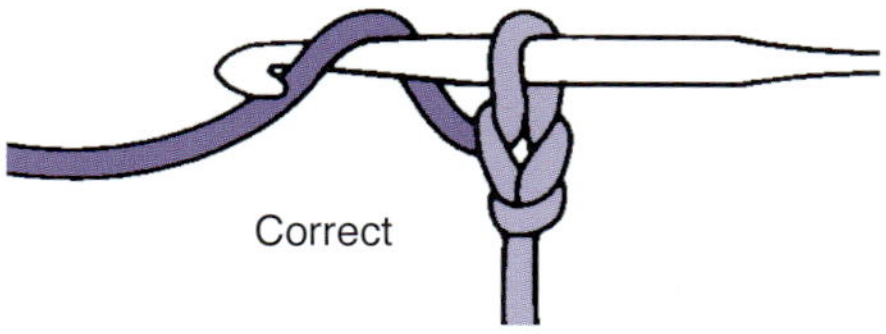

Correct

Fig. 10

***NOTE:** Take care not to bring yarn from front to back (Fig. 11).*

Incorrect

Fig. 11

Hook it and draw through loop on the hook. You have made another chain stitch *(Fig. 12)*.

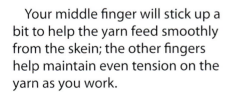

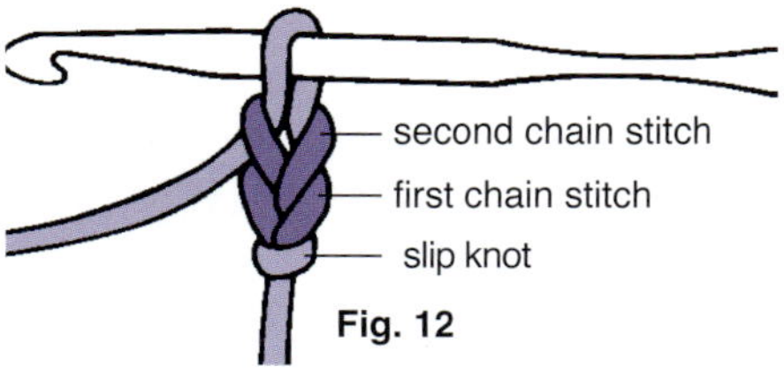

Fig. 12

Repeat step 3 for each additional chain stitch, being careful to move the left thumb and middle or index finger up the chain close to the hook after each new stitch or 2 *(Fig. 13)*. This helps you control the work.

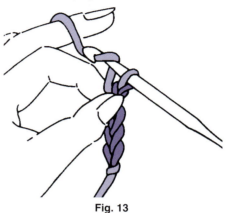

Fig. 13

Also, be sure to pull each new chain up onto the working area of the hook. The working yarn and the work in progress are always held in your left hand.

In the beginning your work will be uneven, with some chain stitches loose and others tight. While you're learning, try to keep the chain stitches loose. As your skill increases, the chain should be firm—but not tight—with all chain stitches even in size.

***HINT:** As you practice, if the hook slips out of a stitch, don't get upset! Just insert the hook again from the front into the center of the last stitch, taking care not to twist the loop (Fig. 14).*

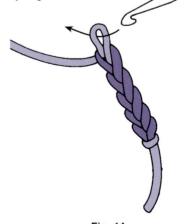

Fig. 14

When you are comfortable with the chain stitch, draw your hook out of the last stitch and pull out the work back to the beginning. Now you've learned the important first step of crochet: the beginning chain.

Parts of the Chain

A chain stitch has three parts: a front loop, a back loop and a back bar.

The front and back loops look like a row of V's *(Fig. 15)*.

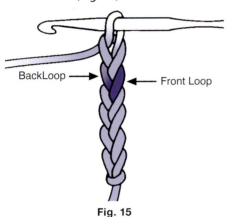

Fig. 15

When the chain is placed on a table with the V shape touching the table, a row of little bumps, like frogs on a log, can be seen. Those bumps are called the back bar *(Fig. 16)*. In the patterns in this book, you will be directed to work in the back bar *(or bump)* because it produces a nice finished edge.

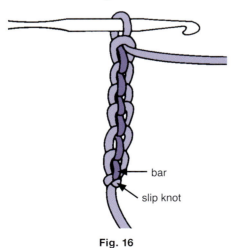

Fig. 16

When counting chains, you will not count the loop on your hook nor the starting loop *(Fig. 17)*.

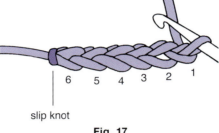

Fig. 17

HOW TO FINISH A CROCHET PROJECT

When your project is complete, fasten off by cutting the yarn, leaving a 5-inch strand. Pull the loop on the hook up until the end of the strand pops through. With a tapestry needle, weave the ending yarn strand, as well as any other loose strands, into the crocheted piece.

To weave in the ends, thread the yarn tail onto the tapestry needle.

Step 1: Turn your work to the wrong side *(the side you don't want people to see)* and run the needle under the V of the stitches for about 1–2 inches, and then pull the yarn through. Do not pull tightly. Give the fabric a little tug widthwise to keep the tension even.

Step 2: Skip over one portion of the V of the stitch and then run the needle and yarn back through the stitches in the opposite direction, again being careful not to pull tightly.

Step 3: Cut the yarn near the fabric.

FINISHED MEASUREMENTS

The finished measurements listed in each pattern are the measurements your piece should be close to once completed. Measurements are given in this book only to show the finished size of the projects in the photos. Since people have different tensions when crocheting, your project may be larger or smaller than the finished measurements given. That is fine. These projects were designed so that end results with different sizes will still work as intended. ●

Chains of Love Heart

Start your crochet journey by creating a long length of the most basic crochet stitch: the chain stitch. Then with a little patience and some wire, you can create this unique heart for your wall.

Finished Measurements
7 inches wide x 6½ inches tall

Materials
- At least 150 yds of smooth, light colored worsted-weight acrylic yarn
- Red Heart Super Saver medium (worsted) weight acrylic yarn (7 oz/364 yds/198g per skein): 1 skein #0259 flamingo

Look for the #4 icon on the label. #4 is used to label worsted-weight yarns.

4 MEDIUM

Yarn used in the sample project is

This is the exact color number and name used so that you can use the same yarn if you would like.

Supplies in Project Bag
- Size 5mm crochet hook (which can also be listed as size H or 8)
- Tapestry needle
- Scissors
- Tape measure
- Locking stitch markers

Additional Items
- 9mm round jump ring in color of choice (only needed if planning to hang the heart on a wall)
- 16-gauge wire, 28 inches long
- If you would like to use the same wire as in the project, it was made with:
  Fire Mountain Gems and Beads Wrap It jeweler's bronze 16-gauge wire H20-2424WR

Optional But Very Helpful Tools
- Needle-nose pliers
- Small wire cutter

Gauge
Gauge is not critical for this project.

Gauge is the number of stitches the designer worked over a specific measurement. To achieve the finished measurements of a pattern, you will need to match these numbers. For this book, designs were intentionally chosen so that gauge does not need to be matched for the first few projects.

Chains of Love Heart Heart Template

Pattern Note
This project is created by making a series of chain stitches and then threading them onto the wire in a specific way.

Skills Needed
- Hold your hook and yarn.
- Put yarn on your hook (using a slip knot or twisting).
- Chain.
- Identify the back bar of the chain.
- Weave in yarn ends.

HEART
Chains
Place a twisted loop or slip knot on hook leaving a 5-inch tail.

Make chain stitches until piece measures about 20 feet long.

Remove loop from hook then place stitch marker in loop to keep chain from unraveling.

Attaching Wire
Bend bottom 3 inches of wire 90 degrees to keep chains on wire.

Hold wire vertically with chain stitches to right of wire.

With **back bar of chains** (see page 6) facing you, push back bar of first chain onto wire.

Skip next 4 back bars.

Moving chains to left of wire, push back bar of next chain onto wire.

Skip next 4 back bars.

Moving chains to right of wire, push back bar of next chain onto wire.

PART ONE

Learn to Crochet: A Beginner's Guide — Chains of Love Heart

Continue moving chains back and forth skipping 4 back bars and pushing back bar of next chain onto wire until all chains are used.

If needed, add or subtract chains so that last chain is on wire and so that chains can be pushed together leaving 3 inches of wire at each end.

When finished filling wire with chains, cut yarn leaving a 5-inch strand.

Remove stitch marker.

Bend top 3 inches of wire 90 degrees to keep chains on wire.

With tapestry needle, weave in yarn ends.

Shaping Heart

Gently bend wire in half to find center of wire.

Using Heart Template for guide, place bent center of wire at bottom of heart then bend remaining wire into heart shape.

With your hands or needle-nose pliers, twist and bend the 3-inch ends together to close top of heart.

Reshape heart if altered during closing.

Remaining ends of wire can be hidden behind project or trimmed with wire cutters.

Adjust chain stitches on heart shape so that wire doesn't show. ●

DID YOU KNOW?
According to Guiness World Records, as of 2021, the record for longest crochet chain is 214.8 miles!

Part Two

TENSION ON FOUNDATION CHAINS

Chain stitches tend to be a bit smaller than other stitches, so it is important to make your foundation chain stitches a little bit loose. When chain stitches are loose, it is easier to insert your hook into them. A loose foundation chain will also keep your foundation row from drawing in so that your beginning foundation row and your last row will be the same length.

Hint: If your tension is tight, one way to help is to work your chain stitches with a hook one size larger than what you plan to use on the project. Then, before starting to work into the chain stiches, change to your project hook.

SINGLE CROCHET (ABBREVIATED SC)

How to Make a Single Crochet in a Chain Stitch

After you have made your loose foundation chain you can start working stitches into the chain. To make a stitch into the chain you can insert your hook in the front loop, back loop, back bar or a combination of any 2 parts of the chain. If it makes a difference to the project, your pattern will tell you which to work into. Otherwise, use whichever loop you prefer. Most projects in this book will request that the stitches be worked in the back bar for 2 reasons:

Step 1. When working stitches in the back bar, the V shape that you see on the top of your stitches will also be on the bottom of the beginning foundation chain, making the top and bottom of your piece match.

Step 2. If pieces are to be sewn together, the V shape on the bottom of the beginning foundation chain provides a front loop and back loop so that an invisible seam can be sewn.

You will never work into the first chain from the hook. Depending on the stitch, you will work into the 2nd, 3rd, 4th, etc., chain from the hook. The instructions will always state in which chain you will work.

Step 1: When working a single crochet into the back bar of the chain, turn your chain over so the smooth side is facing away from you. Find the second bump from the hook, insert hook from front to back through the back bar or bump.

Step 2: Bring the yarn up over the top of your hook.

Step 3: Rotate the hook, pulling the yarn through the bump and bringing the new loop up onto your hook and moving it onto the wider area of the hook. This sizes your stitches. You should now have 2 loops on your hook.

Step 4: Yarn over.

Step 5: Rotating your hook and pulling the yarn through both loops on your hook at the same time. This completes the single crochet.

You will work in each chain but not into the slip knot.

Learn to Crochet: A Beginner's Guide

Finding the First Single Crochet Stitch When Working the Next Row

Crochet stitches have 2 loops at the top which form a horizontal V shape. After you make your first single crochet stitch in the foundation chain, insert a stitch marker through those 2 horizontal loops so that you will be able to find that stitch when working the next row.

It's also helpful to mark the last stitch of the row in the same way when you are just learning. This makes identification of the first and last stitches much easier and you won't lose or miss these stitches as you work.

How to Turn Work

Once you have worked a single crochet stitch in each of the foundation chain stitches, you can turn your work and begin working single crochet stitches into single crochet stitches.

Unless the pattern tells you to turn the project in a particular direction, clockwise or counterclockwise, you can turn your work in whichever direction you prefer. Just be consistent and do the turn the same way each time.

After you turn your work, make one chain and you are ready to start the next row. The chain made before beginning the next row does not count as a stitch. It is called the turning chain and is only made so that the yarn is at the right height to make the first single crochet stitch on the next row. It is marked here with the stitch marker.

How to Make a Single Crochet in a Single Crochet Stitch

Step 1: Make your single crochet stitch by inserting your hook under both loops forming the V shape at the top of the single crochet stitch you are working into.

Step 2: Bring yarn up over the back of the hook *(this is called a yarn over)*. Then, rotate your hook and draw the yarn through the stitch.

Step 3: Yarn over the hook again. Rotate your hook and draw the yarn through both loops on your hook to complete the single crochet.

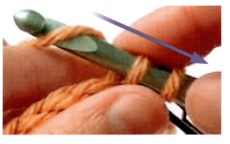

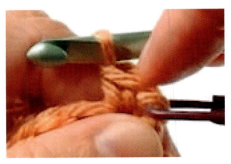

Continuing to work a single crochet into each stitch will produce a nice solid fabric. The uniformity of your stitches will come with time and practice.

How to Tell Right Side From Wrong Side

Row 1 on a pattern is presumed to be the right side *(or the side you want to be seen)* unless the pattern says different. This being the case, if you are not sure if you are working a right-side or a wrong-side *(the side you don't want to be seen)* row, look at your beginning foundation chain yarn strand. If the strand is on your left, you are working a right-side row. If the strand is on your right, you are working a wrong-side row. This is if you are a right-handed crocheter.

***HINT:** If you are concerned you will have trouble telling right from wrong side, place a stitch marker in the front center of your first row to mark the right side.*

HELP FOR LEFT-HANDERS

For left-handed people in a predominantly right-handed world, crocheting can be a very frustrating experience!

Finding information to help left-handed crocheters is difficult, mostly because not a lot of things have been written specifically for left-handed people.

One of the most popular methods for teaching a left-handed person to crochet is for the left-hander to sit directly across from a right-hander or to watch a right-hander in a mirror. Learning to crochet when you are left-handed can be as simple as anything else you are trying to learn, as long as you have the correct instructions. As with any new skill you are trying to learn and be successful at, practice makes perfect. Expect that, as with anything new, it might feel awkward at first to try and manipulate the hook and the yarn. Whether you are left-handed or right-handed, practicing your newly learned skill can be the most important thing to the success of crocheting.

Getting Started

How you will hold your crochet hook is the first thing you will want to determine. Your hook will be held in your left hand and the yarn will be held in, and manipulated by, your right hand. There are two most commonly used ways to hold the crochet hook. The first is called the pencil hold, where you will hold the crochet hook between your thumb and index finger. The second is called the knife hold, where you grip the crochet hook in much the same manner as you would hold a knife. *(See the photos of these two types of hook holds on page 3).*

It is up to you to determine which hold feels more comfortable as there is no correct or incorrect way to hold the hook.

Just as there are different ways to hold your hook, there are also different ways to hold the yarn. The most widely accepted way, though, is to loop the yarn over the middle or index finger of your right hand, holding it loosely across the hand. With your yarn, make a slip knot on your hook.

Hold the slip knot in your right hand between your thumb and middle finger. The yarn will come out between the hook and your index finger. Use your index finger to keep the yarn tight to create an even tension, which is very important if you want to maintain even stitches. You will work the stitches in the same manner as described in this book, just with the opposite hands.

Differences Between Left- & Right-Handed Crocheters

Here are some very important differences to remember about left-handed crochet.

When working back and forth in rows, left-handed crocheters work their stitches from left to right, and right-handed crocheters work from right to left.

When working in rounds, left-handed crocheters work to the right *(clockwise)* and right-handed crocheters work to the left *(counterclockwise)*.

When working back and forth in rows, the finished crochet project will look exactly the same for both right- and left-handed crocheters, except for where the work was started and fastened off *(ended)*.

When working in rounds, the finished crochet project will look different for left- and right-handed crocheters because the stitches will be worked in opposite directions.

The majority of adjustments that left-handed crocheters will have to make will be in reading and interpreting the charts used in crochet. Fortunately, there are no charts used in the patterns in this book.

Most crochet instructions written today are suitable for both right- and left-handed crocheters. The majority of patterns that will need to be amended will be for clothing. But occasionally you will need to reverse instructions for other crochet patterns as well. An example of instructions needing adjusted for a non-clothing item might read, "Join yarn in upper right-hand corner." In this case, you would adjust to join the yarn in the upper left-hand corner. ●

Pretty Bow

Practice your chain stitches and single crochet by making simple little rectangles in pretty colors, then turn them into supercute hair accessories.

Finished Measurements
3½ inches long x 2 inches tall before attaching to elastic

Materials
- At least 10 yds of smooth, light colored worsted-weight polyester or acrylic yarn for each bow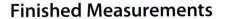
- Lion Brand 42pc Mini Yarn Sampler medium (worsted) weight polyester yarn (⅓ oz/ 22 yds/10g per skein):
    1 skein each of aqua, gray, pink, orange and rose

Supplies in Project Bag
- Size 5mm crochet hook (which can also be listed as size H or 8)
- Tapestry needle
- Scissors
- Tape measure
- Locking stitch markers

Additional Item
- Hair elastics

Gauge
Gauge is not critical for this project.

Pattern Note
To create this little bow, you will make a simple rectangle. You will then wrap yarn around center of rectangle and elastic to create a bow shape.

Skills Needed
- Make a loose foundation chain (starting chains).
- Single crochet.
- Turn work at end of rows.
- Distinguish right side from wrong side.
- Weave in ends.

BOW

Row 1 (right side): With color of choice, place a twisted loop or slip knot on hook leaving a 5-inch tail.

Make 11 chain stitches.

Turn to work back across foundation chain.

Skip first chain closest to hook.

Single crochet in back bar of next chain *(see page 9)*.

Single crochet in back bar of each remaining chain across.

Turn work.

(10 single crochet)

***Note:** To help with placement and counting, place a removable locking stitch marker under the top 2 horizontal loops of the first and last stitch on the row. Move these markers up as you create each new row. When you are confident you can find the first and last stitch on a row, these end stitch markers can be omitted. To help with keeping track of right-side and wrong-side rows, place an additional stitch marker on the right side of the fabric, and leave it in place until the rectangle is completed.*

Look for the #4 icon on the label. #4 is used to label worsted-weight yarns.

Yarn used in the sample project is:

These are the colors from the sampler used so that you can use the same colors if you would like.

Gauge is the number of stitches the designer worked over a specific measurement. To achieve the finished measurements of a pattern, you will need to match these numbers. For this book, designs were intentionally chosen so that gauge does not need to be matched for the first few projects.

The number in parentheses is the number of stitches you have at the end of the row. It is a good idea to count your stitches for the first few rows and occasionally on later rows to make sure your count stays accurate.

Row 2 (wrong side): Chain 1 to build up the height of your row.

Single crochet in first stitch.

Single crochet in each remaining stitch across.

Turn work.

(10 single crochet)

Repeat row 2 until piece is about 2 inches long, measuring from foundation chain to last row.

Fasten off at end of last row leaving a 5-inch tail.

Remove stitch markers.

With tapestry needle, weave in yarn ends.

Finishing

Cut 30-inch length of yarn in same color.

Scrunch bow together at center. Leaving a 5-inch tail at beginning, tightly tie tail around bow center to hold scrunch in place.

With tapestry needle, weave in 5-inch beginning yarn end.

Hold elastic behind center of bow.

Wrap remainder of yarn tail continuously around bow center and elastic until 5 inches remain.

With tapestry needle, push 5-inch tail back and forth under wraps in back of bow to weave in end. ●

You should still have 10 single crochet stitches.

DID YOU KNOW?

Laura Ingalls Wilder, author of the Little House on the Prairie books, had a daughter, Rose, who was the author of Woman's Day Book of American Needlework. *According to Rose Wilder Lane, Susanna Meredith, in 1847, after seeing nuns teaching children how to crochet, opened the first school for crocheting in Cork, Ireland, to help the Irish people during the potato famine. Queen Victoria graciously accepted a few pieces of their work, instantly making crochet the latest vogue in high society England!*

Learn to Crochet: A Beginner's Guide

Part Three

HOW TO SKIP A STITCH

Stitches can be skipped to make open spaces in your crochet piece. These spaces can be left open to create a different overall look, or pieces of yarn or ribbon can be woven through the openings to add color and style. When skipping a stitch, make one chain then don't work into the stitch below the chain.

HOW TO MAKE A SINGLE CROCHET STITCH IN A CHAIN SPACE

To single crochet in a chain space, insert the hook under all three loops of the chain stitch through the open space below the chain, yarn over the hook, draw the yarn through the open space, yarn over the hook and draw the yarn through both loops on the hook.

WHAT IS GAUGE?

Gauge is determined by measuring a small swatch of crochet work and counting how many stitches and how many rows are in a given number of inches.

For instance, the gauge may be: 14 stitches = 4 inches; 17 rows = 4 inches.

This means that when the stitches going across the row were measured, there were 14 stitches every 4 inches. When the rows were measured, there were 17 rows every 4 inches. Generally, your goal as the stitcher is to match the gauge numbers the pattern states by using a larger or smaller hook to adjust your stitches and rows per inch. If you can only meet one number, usually the stitch number is most important.

HOW TO ADD FRINGE

Cut strands of yarn in the number of pieces and length given in the pattern.

Insert the hook from the back of the crocheted piece to the front through the stitch indicated in pattern.

Place the center of the strands on the hook *(see illustration A)* then draw through the stitch until about an inch has been drawn through *(see illustration B)*.

Wrap the ends of the strands around the hook and draw the ends through the loop on the hook *(see illustration C)*.

Pull the ends of the strands gently to tighten the fringe *(see illustration D)*, then trim as desired. ●

Your number of stitches and rows in a 4-inch measurement may be different from what the pattern states, but don't worry about that now.

The projects in this book are written so that gauge is not extremely important for finished size, but your gauge could affect the amount of yarn needed to finish the project.

If you are uncertain about your gauge, purchase a little more yarn than what is called for in the pattern. If the extra yarn is not needed for the project you are working on you can always use it later in a different project.

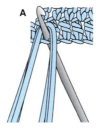 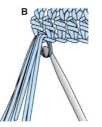  

Fringe

Woven Coaster

Simple crocheted squares become beautiful home decor pieces when worked in pretty color combinations with easy-to-add decorative touches.

Finished Measurement
4 inches square, excluding fringe

Materials
Look for the #4 icon on the label. #4 is used to label worsted-weight yarns.

- At least 60 yds each of smooth worsted-weight cotton yarn in 5 different colors

4 MEDIUM

Yarn used in the sample project is:

- Lily Sugar'n Cream medium (worsted) weight cotton yarn (2½ oz/120 yds/71g per skein):

These are the exact color numbers and names used so that you can use the same yarn if you would like.

   1 skein each #01004 soft ecru, #01042 overcast, #00082 jute, #01152 bamboo and #01153 jade mist

Supplies in Project Bag
- Size 5mm crochet hook (which can also be listed as size H or 8)
- Tapestry needle
- Scissors
- Tape measure
- Locking stitch markers

Gauge
13 stitches = 4 inches;
13 rows = 4 inches

Pattern Note
Coasters are created by first making a square with spaces in the stitching. The optional decorative weaving is then worked through these open spaces in a contrasting color and then contrasting fringe is added in each corner.

Skills Needed
- Make a loose foundation chain.
- Weave in yarn ends.
- Single crochet.
- Tell right side from wrong side.
- Chain 1 to skip a stitch.
- Single crochet in a chain-1 space.
- Make fringe.

Gauge is the number of stitches the designer worked over a specific measurement. To achieve the finished measurements of a pattern, you will need to match these numbers. 13 stitches is what the designer worked over 4 inches using the given yarn and hook in the Materials list. And she achieved 13 rows of stitching over 4 inches. You may need a smaller or larger hook to get the same numbers.

PART THREE

Learn to Crochet: A Beginner's Guide   **Woven Coaster**   15

DID YOU KNOW?
The precursor to crochet was an art called tambouring where crochet chain stitches were worked into material in a similar style to embroidery but using a hook instead of a needle. Modern crochet is worked "in the air," meaning the yarn doesn't have to be attached to any type of material in order for the stitches to be formed.

PART THREE

Place stitch markers in the first and last stitch of each row if you still find this helpful. To help with keeping track of right-side and wrong-side rows, place an additional stitch marker on the right side of the fabric, and leave it in place until the square is completed.

*The * is used to note the start of the stitch repeat. A stitch repeat is a series of stitches worked over and over again across a row of stitches. When a pattern states to repeat from *, this means you go back to the location of the * and work those instructions to the point in the pattern where it states to repeat. Continue working the series: chain 1, skip next stitch, single crochet in next stitch across row.*

On this row the number of stitches, 13 stitches, remains the same, but they are not all the same type of stitches: 7 single crochet + 6 chain-1 spaces = 13 stitches.

This means you will work under the chain-1 into the open space underneath it with your single crochet.

This is a row repeat. Like a stitch repeat that works a series of stitches over and over again, a row repeat works a series of rows over and over again.

COASTER
Make 4.
Choose which of the 5 colors you would like for the fringe, then set that color aside. Make 1 coaster with each of the 4 remaining colors.

Row 1 (right side): With color of choice, place a twisted loop or slip knot on hook leaving a 5-inch tail.

Make 14 chains.

Turn to work back across foundation chain.

Skip first chain closest to hook.

Single crochet in back bar of next chain *(see page 9).*

Single crochet in back bar of each remaining chain across.

Turn work. *(13 single crochet)*

Row 2: Chain 1 to build up the height of your row.

Single crochet in first stitch.

*Chain 1.

Skip next stitch.

Single crochet in next stitch.

Repeat from * across.

Turn work. *(7 single crochet, 6 chain-1 spaces)*

Row 3: Chain 1 to build up the height of your row.

Single crochet in first stitch.

*Single crochet in next chain-1 space.

Single crochet in next stitch.

Repeat from * across.

Turn work. *(13 single crochet)*

Repeat rows 2 and 3 alternately until your piece is a square ending with row 3.

Fasten off at end of last row leaving a 5-inch tail.

Remove stitch markers, if you used them.

With tapestry needle, weave in ends.

Weaving Yarn (Optional)
For each Coaster cut 2 strands of chosen fringe color of yarn 40 inches long.

Place both strands in tapestry needle.

Leaving a 5-inch tail at beginning, draw yarn from back to front through first chain-1 space on bottom right corner.

Weaving from right to left across row, draw yarn from front to back through next chain-1 space.

Continue weaving back and forth across row through each chain-1 space.

After going through last space on row, yarn should be at back of work.

Draw yarn from back to front through chain-1 space 2 rows above current position.

Weave yarn through each chain-1 space across row.

After going through last space on row, yarn should be at back of work.

Continue weaving yarn in established pattern until you have woven yarn through all chain-1 spaces.

Weave in yarn ends.

Corner Fringe
For each Coaster, cut 12 strands of chosen fringe color yarn each 6 inches long. Use 3 6-inch strands per fringe in each corner, referencing fringe instructions *(see page 14)* to complete. ●

Washcloth Pals

After you master creating the pretty stitch pattern in these washcloths, you will learn how to turn them into cute animals with a few additional supplies. Then, you can create a set of these and gift them.

Finished Measurement
10½ inches square

Materials
- At least 180 yds of smooth worsted-weight cotton yarn for each cloth
- Premier Yarns Cotton Sprout Worsted medium (worsted) weight cotton yarn (3½ oz/ 180 yds/100g per skein):
    1 skein for each cloth #07 peach, #08 yellow and #27 beige

4 MEDIUM

Look for the #4 icon on the label. #4 is used to label worsted-weight yarns.

Yarn used in the sample project is:

These are the colors from the sampler used so that you can use the same colors if you would like.

Supplies in Project Bag
- Size 5mm crochet hook (which can also be listed as size H or 8)
- Tapestry needle
- Scissors
- Tape measure
- Locking stitch markers

Additional Items
For Bunny:
1 rubber band
- 18-inch x 7mm ribbon in color of choice

For Bear:
- 1 rubber band
- 18-inch x 9mm ribbon in color of choice

Gauge
11½ stitches = 3 inches; 11½ rows = 3 inches.

Gauge is the number of stitches the designer worked over a specific measurement. To achieve the finished measurements of a pattern, you will need to match these numbers. For this book, designs were intentionally chosen so that gauge does not need to be matched for the first few projects.

Pattern Notes
This washcloth is made by working a simple stitch pattern repeat. A stitch repeat is a series of stitches that you repeat over and over again across a row.

The square washcloth is folded to form the animal shapes.

Skills Needed
- Make a loose foundation chain.
- Work into chains.
- Single crochet.
- Work into single crochet.
- Work into the front or back loop of a stitch.
- Weave in ends.

WASHCLOTH
Bottom Border
Row 1 (foundation—right side): With color of choice, place a twisted loop or slip knot loop on hook leaving a 5-inch tail.

Make 41 chain stitches.

Turn to work back across foundation chain.

Skip first chain closest to hook.

Single crochet in back bar of next chain *(see page 9).*

Single crochet in back bar of each remaining chain across.

Turn work. *(40 single crochet)*

Row 2: Chain 1 to build up the height of your row.

Single crochet in both loops of first stitch.

Single crochet in the **front loop** *(see page 20)* only of each stitch across to last stitch.

Single crochet in both loops of last stitch.

Place stitch markers in the first and last stitch of each row if you still find this helpful. To help with keeping track of right-side and wrong-side rows, place an additional stitch marker on the right side of the fabric, and leave it in place until the square is completed.

The number in parentheses is the number of stitches you have at the end of the row. It is a good idea to count your stitches for the first few rows and occasionally on later rows to make sure your count stays accurate.

This is how you have been working into single crochet stitches to this point in the book.

You should still have 40 single crochet stitches.

To track rows you may find it helpful to keep a scrap of paper nearby to make tally marks and notes on as you complete each section.

*The * is used to note the start of the stitch repeat. Again, a stitch repeat is a series of stitches worked over and over again across a row of stitches. When a pattern states to repeat from *, this means you go back to the location of the * and work those instructions to the point in the pattern where it states to repeat. So, the stitch repeat in this pattern is: single crochet in back loop only of next stitch, single crochet in front loop only of next stitch. This is what is repeated over and over again to the last stitch of the row.*

PART THREE

Turn work. *(40 single crochet)*

Repeat row 2 twice.

You should have a total of 4 rows.

Main Pattern

Row 5: Chain 1 to build up the height of your row.

Single crochet in both loops of first stitch.

*Single crochet in **back loop only** (see page 20) of next stitch.

Single crochet in front loop only of next stitch.

Repeat from * across the row to the last stitch.

Single crochet in both loops of last stitch.

Turn work. *(40 single crochet)*

Measure the width of your last row from first stitch to last stitch.

You need your finished cloth to be a square.

Repeat row 5 until your piece is about ¾ inch less than a square ending after making a right-side row. Your beginning foundation yarn tail will be to your left when you are working a right-side row *(or to your right if crocheting left-handed)*. You might have also marked it with a stitch marker as suggested.

Work row 2 of Border 3 times to make an ending border that matches the beginning border.

Fasten off at end of last row leaving a 5-inch tail.

Remove stitch markers.

With tapestry needle, weave in ends. ●

This means you will go back up to row 2 and repeat it the same number of times you worked it previously to match the end of your square to the start of your square.

DID YOU KNOW?
The art of folding napery, or household linens, can be traced as far back as the 1600s where the most popular styles resembled animals.

FOLDED ANIMALS
Scan this code with your smartphone camera to access your videos.

Washcloth Pals

Part Four

HANKS OF YARN

Yarn can be wound and sold in several different ways. Most commonly you will find them in skeins, balls or cakes. Hanks are generally found in shops that specialize specifically in yarn.

Unlike skeins and cakes, hanks need to be prepared by putting them in ball or cake form before use.

To prepare the yarn, you need to undo the hank and open it up into its full circle. The yarn needs to be placed around something to hold it so that you can wind it into a ball. You can purchase a yarn swift but anything will do—someone's outstretched arms, a chair back or the legs of a flipped-over chair.

Once you place the hank around your preferred surface, you will notice that the strands are being held in place with ties. Cut the ties and remove them. Look for the start of the yarn. Normally it is tied to the end of the yarn. Cut or untie it and you are ready to hand-wind the yarn into balls. This can take a bit of time but is also a nice meditative process.

Start by wrapping the yarn several times around a few of your fingers. Then remove the small wound bit from your fingers and wrap the yarn several times around it. Continue wrapping around the central section. Rotate the ball after every few wraps. This will create a more uniform ball. Do not pull tightly on your yarn when creating the ball. You don't want to wind the ball tightly as this will stretch out your yarn.

SEWING

Sometimes a piece of crochet work needs to be sewn or pieces of crochet work need to be sewn together. A pattern will usually say which sewing method to use, but if no method is given, it is generally presumed that you will whipstitch the pieces together. You can also work seams with an invisible seam or embroidery stitches, like running stitch or backstitch.

How to Whipstitch Pieces Together

Hold the pieces with right sides together and sew through the back loops only *(see Photo A)*. Sewing through the back loops only gives a pretty result, with the unworked loops forming a subtle outline ridge on the right side of the work.

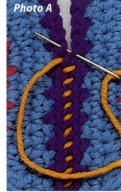
Photo A

If you prefer not to have a ridged outline on the pieces visible on the front side, sew through both loops of the stitches as shown here *(see Photo B)*.

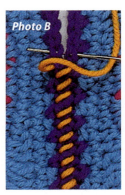
Photo B

Learn to Crochet: A Beginner's Guide

How to Sew an Invisible Seam

Place the pieces to be sewn together side by side with right sides facing up.

Work only through the back loops of each piece.

Push the tapestry needle from right side to wrong side through the bottom stitch on the left piece, then push the needle from right side to wrong side through the bottom stitch on the right piece.

The first stitches are now sewn.

Push the needle from right side to wrong side through the same loop on the left piece as last time, then push the needle from wrong side to right side through the next loop on the left piece.

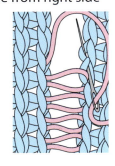

Invisible Seam

Push the needle from right side to wrong side through the same loop on the right piece as last time, then push the needle from wrong side to right side through the next loop on the right piece.

Continue pushing the needle through the loops on the left, then the loops on the right for about 2 inches. Then, pull the end of the yarn strand gently until it disappears into the seam.

Repeat this procedure until all stitches are sewn together.

SINGLE CROCHET IN BOTH LOOPS, FRONT LOOP OR BACK LOOP

When a pattern tells you to single crochet in a stitch, it is understood that you should do this by inserting your hook under both the front and back loop of the stitch you are working into.

However, sometimes a pattern will specifically say to single crochet only in the front loop of a stitch or single crochet only in the back loop of a stitch. This is done to create a different look on your finished piece.

It is important to remember that when you are working a row of stitches, the front loop is always the loop that is closest to you and the back loop is always the loop that is furthest from you. Turning your work at the end of a row does not change this. The front loop is always the loop that is closest to you.

DECORATIVE LITTLE LOOP EDGING

After turning at the end of a row, you make one chain stitch to get your yarn at the right height to single crochet into the next row. This creates a somewhat straight edge on your crochet piece. To make a little decorative loop on the end of your row, you can make 3 chain stitches before starting your next row. ●

Woolly Warmers

Keep your extremities toasty once you learn how to create these simple fingerless mitts and leg warmers. You will want to make a set of each to keep everywhere: in your car, in the office, by the couch, in each of your coats …

PART FOUR

Finished Measurements

Fingerless Mitts: 8 inches long x 7 inches in circumference

Leg Warmers: 14¾ inches long x 13 inches in circumference

Materials

- At least 220 yds of smooth worsted-weight wool yarn for fingerless mitts and at least 440 yds of same yarn for leg warmers
- Premier Yarns Stitch Please medium (worsted) weight wool yarn (3½ oz/220 yds/100g per hank):
  - 1 hank of either #36 salted caramel or #60 gray all day (for fingerless mitts)
  - 2 hanks of either #21 party thyme or #25 rust in the wind (for leg warmers)

4 MEDIUM

Look for the #4 icon on the label. #4 is used to label worsted-weight yarns.

Yarn used in the sample project is:

These are the exact color numbers and names used so that you can use the same yarn if you would like.

Supplies in Project Bag

- Size 5mm crochet hook (which can also be listed as size H or 8)
- Tapestry needle
- Scissors
- Tape measure
- Locking stitch markers

Gauge

14 stitches = 4 inches; 17 rows = 4 inches

Gauge is the number of stitches the designer worked over a specific measurement. To achieve the finished measurements of a pattern, you will need to match these numbers. 14 stitches is what the designer worked over 4 inches using the given yarn and hook in the Materials list. And she achieved 17 rows of stitching over 4 inches. You may need a smaller or larger hook to get the same numbers.

Pattern Notes

To make the fingerless mitts and the leg warmers, the process is very similar. You create a rectangle of stretchy fabric until it can wrap around your hand or lower leg when slightly stretched. Then for the mitts you sew the 2 long sides together, leaving a hole for your thumb. For the leg warmers you will sew the entire length of the sides together.

Skills Needed

- Make a loose foundation chain.
- Weave in yarn ends.
- Single crochet in both loops.
- Turn work.
- Tell right side from wrong side.
- Sew 2 pieces together.
- Single crochet in back loop only.
- Turn work at end of row with a 3-chain loop to create a decorative edge.

WOOLLY WARMERS
Fingerless Mitt
Make 2.

This tells us that to make a set you will need to make 2 pieces following the directions below.

Row 1 (right side): With color of choice, place a twisted loop or slip knot on hook leaving a 10-inch tail for sewing.

Make 28 chains.

Place a stitch marker in **back bar** *(see page 6)* of last chain made.

Make 3 more chains.

Turn to work back across foundation chain.

Single crochet in marked back bar and remove marker.

This is the 4th chain from the hook. The skipped chains will create the first decorative loop on the edge.

Place the stitch marker in stitch just made to mark first stitch.

Single crochet in back bar of each remaining chain across.

Place a stitch marker in stitch just made to mark last stitch.

Turn work. *(28 single crochet, 1 decorative loop)*

The number in parentheses is the number of stitches you have at the end of the row. It is a good idea to count your stitches for the first few rows and occasionally on later rows to make sure your count stays accurate.

Row 2: Chain 3 to form decorative loop.

Single crochet in both loops of marked stitch.

> *You should still have 28 single crochet and 1 decorative loop.*

> *Your beginning foundation yarn tail will be to your right (left if you are crocheting left-handed) when you are working a wrong-side row.*

Turn work. *(28 single crochet, 1 decorative loop)*

Repeat row 2 until piece is about 7 inches long, measuring from foundation chain to last row, or until piece will fit comfortably around hand when lightly stretched, ending with a wrong-side row.

Fasten off at end of last row leaving a tail at least twice as long as the length of your Woolly Warmer for sewing.

Remove stitch markers.

Finishing

Fold piece so that last row and beginning foundation chain are touching, right side is showing and ending tail is at front top right.

On end closest to beginning 10-inch yarn tail, insert stitch marker through both layers in desired location to mark beginning of thumb opening.

Place another stitch marker in desired location for ending thumb opening.

With tapestry needle and ending tail, working through **front loop** *(see page 20)* of single crochet on last row and front loop of chain on foundation chain, **whipstitch** *(see page 19)* across to marked stitch for ending thumb opening.

Turn work so beginning 10-inch tail is at front top right.

With tapestry needle and beginning 10-inch yarn tail, using same method as before, whipstitch across to marked stitch for beginning of thumb opening.

Remove stitch markers.

With tapestry needle, weave in yarn ends.

Remove marker and place it in stitch just made.

Single crochet in **back loop** *(see page 20)* only of each stitch across to marked stitch.

Single crochet in both loops of marked stitch.

Remove marker and place it in stitch just made.

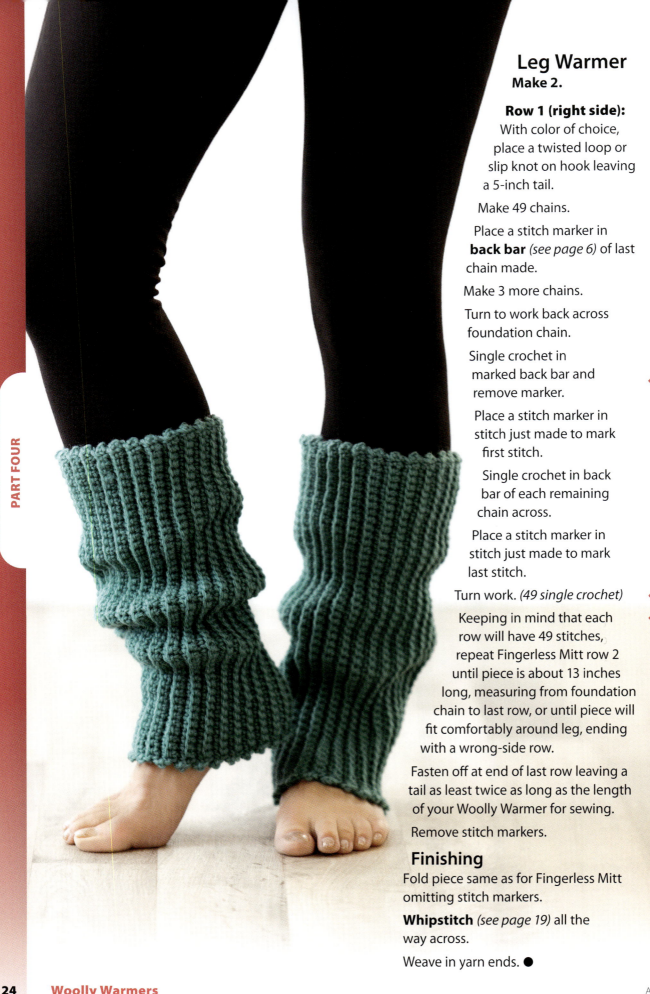

Leg Warmer
Make 2.

Row 1 (right side): With color of choice, place a twisted loop or slip knot on hook leaving a 5-inch tail.

Make 49 chains.

Place a stitch marker in **back bar** *(see page 6)* of last chain made.

This is the 4th chain from the hook. The skipped chains will create the first decorative loop on the edge.

Make 3 more chains.

Turn to work back across foundation chain.

Single crochet in marked back bar and remove marker.

Place a stitch marker in stitch just made to mark first stitch.

Single crochet in back bar of each remaining chain across.

Place a stitch marker in stitch just made to mark last stitch.

Turn work. *(49 single crochet)*

The number in parentheses is the number of stitches you have at the end of the row. It is a good idea to count your stitches for the first few rows and occasionally on later rows to make sure your count stays accurate.

Keeping in mind that each row will have 49 stitches, repeat Fingerless Mitt row 2 until piece is about 13 inches long, measuring from foundation chain to last row, or until piece will fit comfortably around leg, ending with a wrong-side row.

Your beginning foundation yarn tail will be to your right (left if you are crocheting left-handed) when you are working a wrong-side row.

Fasten off at end of last row leaving a tail as least twice as long as the length of your Woolly Warmer for sewing.

Remove stitch markers.

Finishing
Fold piece same as for Fingerless Mitt omitting stitch markers.

Whipstitch *(see page 19)* all the way across.

Weave in yarn ends. ●

Part Five

PATTERN INFORMATION & ABBREVIATIONS

Since all projects are started by placing a twisted loop or slip knot *(loop)* on the hook and leaving a beginning 5-inch strand, this information is generally not written at the start of a pattern. Nor is the information about leaving a 5-inch strand at the end when cutting the yarn. Starting with this section and going forward, this information will be omitted from the patterns in this book. The length of beginning and ending yarn strands will only be included if extra length is needed for sewing.

Since it is understood that the number in parentheses at the end of a row tells how many stitches are on that row, that explanation will also be omitted.

The suggestion to place a stitch marker in the first and last stitch is not something you have to do unless you need help finding the first and last stitch, so that explanation will be left out of the patterns going forward as well. Keep in mind that occasionally a pattern will specifically say to place a stitch marker in a certain stitch. Those stitch markers are generally not optional as they mark a spot that you will need to be able to find later.

Counting the stitches on your row to make sure you haven't missed a stitch is always a good idea.

Occasionally measuring your piece to make sure it is close to the finished size you need is also a good idea.

Also beginning with this section, although all words will continue to be written out, standard crochet abbreviations will be written in parentheses following the spelled-out words.

HOW TO JOIN A NEW COLOR ON A ROW

Insert your hook under the top 2 loops of the stitch where the new color is to be joined. With the new color, leaving a 5-inch strand at the beginning, yarn over the hook.

Draw the yarn through the stitch.

Then chain 1. The chain-1 will join your yarn and will also count as the beginning chain-1 to build up the height of your row.

After you make your first single crochet, in the same stitch where the join was made, you might notice that the beginning strand is a little loose. Not to worry, you will weave it in later and tight the stitch back up in the process.

HOW TO DECREASE AT THE BEGINNING OF A ROW

To decrease at the beginning of a row when working single crochet stitches, make your beginning chain 1 to build up the height of your row, skip the first stitch on the row.

Single crochet in the 2nd stitch on the row.

By skipping the first stitch on the row, you have decreased the number of stitches on the row by one.

HOW TO WHIPSTITCH PIECES ON TOP OF PIECES

When whipstitching a crochet piece on top of another crochet piece, where each piece is a different color, use a yarn strand the same color as the top piece to make the whipstitches.

When making the whipstitches, insert the tapestry needle only under one strand on the bottom piece, then insert the tapestry needle through the edge of the top piece so that the top color of yarn doesn't show on the back side of the bottom piece. This will give your finished piece a more professional look when working on a project where the back of the bottom piece will also be seen. ●

Mini Monster Pouch

We think you are going to have a lot of fun creating a mini monster pouch. Mix and match colors and different pieces to create a truly unique little pouch.

Finished Measurements
6¼ inches wide x 5¼ inches tall, excluding strap

Materials
- For each pouch: At least 170 yds of smooth worsted-weight acrylic yarn for pouch and at least 50 yds each in 4 additional colors for embellishments
- Lion Brand Yarn Vanna's Choice medium (worsted) weight acrylic/rayon yarn (3½ oz/170 yds/100g per skein):
  1 skein each #101A pink, #178AC sea glass, #100 white, #146I dusty purple and #158I mustard

Supplies in Project Bag
- Size 5mm crochet hook (which can also be listed as size H or 8)
- Tapestry needle
- Scissors
- Tape measure
- Locking stitch markers

Additional Items for Each Pouch
- 22mm black shank buttons: 2 for eyes
- 12mm white plastic rings: 2 to attach strap

Gauge
16 stitches (sts) = 5 inches; 19 rows = 5 inches

Gauge is the number of stitches (sts) the designer worked over a specific measurement. To achieve the finished measurements of a pattern, you will need to match these numbers. 16 stitches (sts) is what the designer worked over 5 inches using the given yarn and hook in the Materials list. And she achieved 19 rows of stitching over 5 inches. You may need a smaller or larger hook to get the same numbers.

Pattern Note
The pouch itself is created by working a rectangle of single crochet stitches that is then folded up and sewn in place to form the sides. Then, you can create the features of your choice to embellish your monster pouch.

Skills Needed
- Make a loose foundation chain.
- Weave in yarn ends.
- Single crochet.
- Tell right side from wrong side.
- Join pieces with whipstitch.
- Understand gauge.
- Join a new color on row.
- Decrease at beginning of row.
- Whipstitch pieces on top of other pieces.
- Tie overhand knot.

POUCH
Row 1 (right side {RS}): With color of choice, make 21 chains (chs).

Turn to work back across foundation chain (ch).

Skip (sk) first chain (ch) closest to hook.

Single crochet (sc) in back bar of next chain (ch) (see page 9).

Single crochet (sc) in back bar of each remaining (rem) chain (ch) across.

Turn work. *(20 single crochet {sc})*

Row 2: Chain (ch) 1.

Single crochet (sc) in first stitch (st).

Single crochet (sc) in each remaining (rem) stitch (st) across.

Turn work. *(20 single crochet {sc})*

Repeat (rep) row 2 until piece is about 13½ inches long, measuring from foundation chain (ch) to last row, ending with a wrong-side (WS) row.

When a pattern starts with making chains (chs), start with a twisted loop or slip knot on the hook.

Mini Monster Pouch   27

Your beginning *(beg)* foundation yarn tail will be to your right when you are working a wrong-side *(WS)* row *(left when crocheting left-handed)*.

Fasten off at end of last row.

Gums

With right side *(RS)* facing,

beginning *(beg)* foundation yarn tail will be to your left,

join your chosen gum color yarn in first stitch *(st)* on the last row.

Do this by inserting your hook under top 2 loops *(lps)* of first stitch *(st)*, draw new color yarn through stitch *(st)* then chain *(ch)* 1.

Single crochet *(sc)* in same stitch *(st)* as joining.

Single crochet *(sc)* in each stitch *(st)* across row.

Do not turn work.

Fasten off. *(20 single crochet {sc})*

Teeth

Choose if you want your Monster to have 6, 4 or 2 teeth, then follow directions for How to Make a Tooth.

For Six Teeth: With right side *(RS)* facing, skip *(sk)* first stitch *(st)* on row, make 6 teeth going across row, leave last stitch *(st)* unworked.

For Four Teeth: With right side *(RS)* facing, skip *(sk)* first stitch *(st)* on row, make tooth. *Skip *(sk)* next 2 stitches *(sts)* then make a tooth. Repeat *(rep)* from * for each remaining *(rem)* tooth. Leave last stitch *(st)* unworked.

For Two Teeth: With right side *(RS)* facing, skip *(sk)* first 5 stitches *(sts)* on row, make tooth, skip *(sk)* next 4 stitches *(sts)* on row, make tooth, leave last 5 stitches *(sts)* unworked.

How to Make a Tooth

Row 1 (right side {RS}): Join your chosen tooth color yarn in gum colored stitch *(st)* where you want your tooth to start,

Single crochet *(sc)* in same stitch *(st)* as joining.

Single crochet *(sc)* in next 2 stitches *(sts)*.

Turn work. *(3 single crochet {sc})*

Row 2: Chain *(ch)* 1.

skip *(sk)* first stitch *(st)* to decrease *(dec)*.

Single crochet *(sc)* in next stitch *(st)*.

Single crochet *(sc)* in last stitch *(st)*.

Turn work. *(2 single crochet {sc})*

Row 3: Chain *(ch)* 1.

Skip *(sk)* first stitch *(st)* to decrease *(dec)*.

Single crochet *(sc)* in last stitch *(st)*.

Fasten off. *(1 single crochet {sc})*

Closing Sides

Place piece on table with wrong side *(WS)* touching table.

Fold bottom foundation row up 4¾ inches then fold top of piece down over foundation row.

Adjust folds as needed so teeth do not go past bottom of pouch.

Unfold top of pouch.

Place a stitch marker or 2 on sides to hold bottom fold in place.

Cut 1 24-inch strand of matching pouch color yarn for each side.

With tapestry needle and strand, whipstitch each side closed.

Turn pouch right side *(RS)* out so whipstitch seams are on inside of pouch.

Remove all stitch markers and weave in all yarn ends.

Face

Choose which colors and shapes you would like for your mini monster's face.

After desired shapes are crocheted, with tapestry needle and matching color yarn strand, sew button eyes onto shapes if a shape is wanted behind eye, then whipstitch shapes and or eyes onto pouch. Weave in all yarn ends.

If you would like to use the same colors and shapes as in the project, they were made as follows:

Dusty purple pouch has mustard triangle eye and seaglass bitten diamond eye.

Seaglass pouch has pink bitten diamond eye and dusty purple bow.

Pink pouch has dusty purple triangle nose and mustard bow.

Bitten Diamond Shape

Row 1 (right side {RS}): With color of choice, make 7 chains (chs).

Turn to work back across foundation chain (ch).

Skip (sk) first chain (ch) closest to hook.

Single crochet (sc) in back bar of next chain (ch).

Single crochet (sc) in back bar of each remaining (rem) chain (ch) across.

Turn work. *(6 single crochet {sc})*

Row 2: Chain (ch) 1.

Single crochet (sc) in first stitch (st).

Single crochet (sc) in each remaining (rem) stitch (st) across.

Turn work. *(6 single crochet {sc})*

Rows 3–5: Repeat (rep) row 2.

Row 6: Chain (ch) 1.

Single crochet (sc) in first stitch (st).

Single crochet (sc) in next 3 stitches (sts).

Leave last 2 stitches (sts) unworked for bite mark.

Fasten off leaving a 20-inch tail for sewing. *(4 single crochet {sc})*

Weave in beginning (beg) yarn end.

Triangle Shape

Row 1 (right side {RS}): With color of choice, make 7 chains (chs).

Turn to work back across foundation chain (ch).

Skip (sk) first chain (ch) closest to hook.

Single crochet (sc) in back bar of next chain (ch).

Single crochet (sc) in back bar of each remaining (rem) chain (ch) across.

Turn work. *(6 single crochet {sc})*

Row 2: Chain (ch) 1.

Skip (sk) first stitch (st) to decrease (dec).

Single crochet (sc) in next stitch (st).

Single crochet (sc) in each remaining (rem) stitch (st) across.

Turn work. *(5 single crochet {sc})*

Rows 3–5: Repeat (rep) row 2.

Last row will have 2 single crochet (sc).

Row 6: Chain (ch) 1.

Skip (sk) first stitch (st) to decrease (dec).

Single crochet (sc) in last stitch (st). *(1 single crochet {sc})*

Fasten off leaving a 20-inch tail for sewing.

Weave in beginning (beg) yarn end.

Bow Shape

(Right Side {RS}): With color of choice, make 21 chains (chs).

Turn to work back across foundation chain (ch).

Skip (sk) first chain (ch) closest to hook.

Single crochet *(sc)* in back bar of next chain *(ch)*.

Single crochet *(sc)* in back bar of each remaining *(rem)* chain *(ch)* across. *(20 single crochet {sc})*

Fasten off leaving a 20-inch tail for sewing.

Weave in beginning *(beg)* yarn end.

With tapestry needle and ending yarn tail, whipstitch first and last stitch *(st)* together *(tog)* to form a ring.

Flatten ring with seam at center back.

Wrap tail around center of piece 3 times to form middle of bow.

Push tapestry needle around wraps in back of bow to hold wraps in place.

Strap

Choose which colors you would like for your strap.

If you would like to use the same colors as in the project, they were made as follows:

Dusty purple pouch 2 strands of each of the 5 colors.

Sea glass pouch 5 strands dusty purple and 5 strands sea glass.

Pink pouch 10 strands pink.

Cut 10 strands of yarn 70 inches long in colors of choice.

Draw first 7 inches of all strands through 12mm ring and tie in overhand knot to attach strands to ring.

Holding all strands together *(tog)*, tie overhand knot about every 2 inches until strap is 2 inches less than desired length.

Draw end of strands through next 12mm ring, tie strands in overhand knot to attach strands to ring about 2 inches from last knot.

Cut a 14-inch strand of yarn same color as pouch.

With tapestry needle, and 14-inch yarn strand, whipstitch 12mm ring to each side of pouch at top of side seam making enough whipstitches to cover ring.

Trim fringe ears to desired length. ●

> **DID YOU KNOW?**
> Although time may prove them not to be the first, written crochet patterns have been found as far back as the 1820s. The directions were for 3 crocheted pouches and were published in a Dutch magazine called *Penélopé*.

PART FIVE

Mini Monster Pouch

Part Six

OTHER STITCHES

The single crochet stitch is just one of many stitches that can be made with a crochet hook. After learning a few other stitches, you will be able to crochet them individually or combine them to make an unlimited number of textures.

Half Double Crochet (abbreviated hdc)

This stitch is the next stitch up in height from a single crochet. It is basically working half of a double crochet stitch *(described in Part Seven)*.

How to Make a Half Double Crochet in a Chain Stitch

Step 1: Yarn over the hook from back to front.

Skip one or 2 back bar of chain(s) depending on pattern instructions then insert the hook in the 2nd or 3rd chain from the hook. Each designer has their own preference here.

***NOTE:** You can work through different portions of the chain stitch, but in this book we are working into the back bar of the chains.*

Remember not to count the loop on the hook as a chain and to always bring the loops up onto the working portion of the hook as this is what sizes your stitches.

Step 2: Yarn over the hook from back to front and draw it through the chain stitch and up onto the working area of the hook *(3 loops on hook)*.

Step 3: Yarn over the hook from back to front and draw it through all 3 loops on the hook in one motion.

You have completed one half double crochet; one loop remains on the hook.

For the next stitch, yarn over the hook from back to front and go into the next back bar of chain and then repeat steps 2 and 3. Repeat in each remaining chain across.

After you turn your work, make 1 or 2 chain(s) and you are ready to start the next row. The beginning chain(s) may or may not count as a stitch. Your pattern will specify this information. This is called the turning chain and is only made so that the yarn is at the right height to make the first half double crochet stitch on the next row.

How to Make a Half Double Crochet in a Stitch

Work the first stitch where directed in the pattern.

Step 1: Yarn over the hook from back to front, then insert the hook under the top 2 loops of the stitch.

Step 2: Yarn over the hook from back to front, then draw it through the stitch.

Learn to Crochet: A Beginner's Guide

Step 3: Yarn over the hook from back to front, then draw it through all 3 loops on the hook.

You will work half double crochet in this manner across all stitches.

The 3 Loops of a Half Double Crochet

Half double crochet stitches are a unique stitch in that they not only have a top horizontal front and back loop, but they also have a 3rd loop underneath the top 2 loops. The 3rd loop, or back bar, is formed when the yarn is placed over the hook before inserting the hook into the stitch.

Just like single crochet, if the pattern doesn't say otherwise, it is always assumed that the half double crochet stitch will be worked by inserting the hook under the top horizontal front and back loop of the stitch. To create different textures with half double crochet stitches, you may be directed to work in any of these 3 locations.

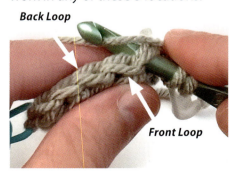

Back Loop
Front Loop

Back Bar

How to Make an Invisible Half Double Crochet Decrease

Step 1: Yarn over the hook from back to front, insert the hook in the back bar.

Step 2: Then insert your hook in the next back bar *(4 loops on hook)*.

Step 3: Yarn over the hook from back to front, draw yarn through first 2 loops on hook *(3 loops on hook)*.

Step 4: Yarn over hook from back to front, draw through all 3 loops on the hook.

HOW TO INCREASE

To increase the number of stitches you have on your row, work 2 stitches into the same stitch. ●

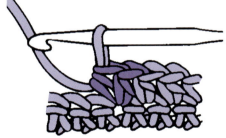

half double crochet increase

PART SIX

Mystical Halves Scarf

A fun two-color repeating texture is divided by thin strips of color and accented with cute little pompoms in this pretty scarf.

Finished Measurements
12 inches wide x 78 inches long

Materials
- At least 850 yds of smooth worsted-weight acrylic yarn for body of scarf, plus 320 yds for ends and 200 yds for contrasting stripes
- Red Heart Soft medium (worsted) weight acrylic yarn (5 oz/256 yds/141g per skein):
    - 4 skeins #9520 seafoam for body
    - 2 skeins #4601 off white for ends
    - 1 skein #9518 teal for stripes

Supplies in Project Bag
- Size 5mm crochet hook (which can also be listed as size H or 8)
- Tapestry needle
- Scissors
- Tape measure

Optional Items
- 22mm shank buttons: 2

Gauge
17 stitches (sts) = 4 inches;
10 rows = 4 inches

Pattern Notes
Scarf is worked from one short end to opposite short end. Then pompoms are added at the end for a decorative touch. An optional way of attaching pompoms is stated at the ended for those wishing to be able to remove them from time to time.

Chain-1 at beginning of row does not count as a stitch.

Gauge is the number of stitches (sts) the designer worked over a specific measurement. To achieve the finished measurements of a pattern, you will need to match these numbers. 17 stitches (sts) is what the designer worked over 4 inches using the given yarn and hook in the Materials list. And she achieved 10 rows of stitching over 4 inches. You may need a smaller or larger hook to get the same numbers.

Learn to Crochet: A Beginner's Guide

Skills Needed
- Make a loose foundation chain.
- Weave in yarn ends.
- Turn counterclockwise.
- Tell right side from wrong side.
- Join a new color on a row.
- Half double crochet.
- Identify 3 horizontal loops of a half double crochet.
- Work an invisible half double crochet decrease.
- Increase.
- Make a pompom.
- Identify back bar of chain.

SCARF
Scarf Beginning (Beg)
Row 1 (right side {RS}): With off white,

make 51 chains *(chs)*.

Turn to work back across foundation chain *(ch)*.

Skip *(sk)* first chain *(ch)* closest to hook.

Half double crochet *(hdc)* in back bar of next chain *(ch)* *(see page 31)* and of each remaining *(rem)* chain *(ch)* across.

Turn work.

(50 half double crochet {hdc})

Row 2: Chain (ch) 1 *(see Pattern Notes).*

Half double crochet *(hdc)* in **back loop (lp)** *(see page 32)* of first stitch *(st)*.

Half double crochet *(hdc)* in back loop *(lp)* of next stitch *(st)*.

*****Half double crochet (hdc) in back bar** *(see page 32)* of next 2 stitches *(sts)*.

Half double crochet *(hdc)* in back loop *(lp)* of next 2 stitches *(sts)*.

Repeat *(rep)* from * across row.

Turn work.

> *This means you will go back to the point where the * is and work the instructions from that point to before the word repeat (rep) over and over again until you have worked across all stitches (sts).*

(50 half double crochet {hdc})

Row 3: Chain *(ch)* 1.

Half double crochet *(hdc)* in back bar of first stitch *(st)*.

Half double crochet *(hdc)* in back bar of next stitch *(st)*.

*Half double crochet *(hdc)* in back loop *(lp)* of next 2 stitches *(sts)*.

Half double crochet *(hdc)* in back bar of next 2 stitches *(sts)*.

Repeat *(rep)* from * across row.

Turn work.

(50 half double crochet {hdc})

Repeat *(rep)* rows 2 and 3 until piece is about 9 inches long, measuring from foundation chain *(ch)* to last row and ending with a wrong side *(WS)* row 2.

Fasten off at end of last row.

Contrasting Stripe
Row 1 (right side {RS}): Join teal *(see page 25)* in back bar of first stitch *(st)*.

Half double crochet *(hdc)* in back bar of first stitch *(st)* *(this is the same stitch {st} you pulled the new loop {lp} of yarn through)*.

Half double crochet *(hdc)* in back bar of next 2 stitches *(sts)*.

*Work invisible **half double crochet decrease *(inv hdc dec)*** *(see page 32)* in back bar of next 2 stitches *(sts)*.

Half double crochet *(hdc)* in back bar of next 4 stitches *(sts)*.

Repeat *(rep)* from * to last 5 stitches *(sts)*.

Invisible half double crochet decrease *(inv hdc dec)* in back bar of next 2 stitches *(sts)*.

Half double crochet *(hdc)* in back bar of last 3 stitches *(sts)*.

Turn work.

Mystical Halves Scarf

> **DID YOU KNOW?**
> A Nigerian woman, Chidinma Modupe Okafor, holds the record for crocheting without stopping. She worked for 72 consecutive hours to create a white dinner gown.

> *On the last row you crocheted 2 stitches (sts) together (tog) a total of 8 times so you now have 42 half double crochet (hdc) stitches (sts) on your row.*

(42 half double crochet {hdc})

Row 2: Chain (ch) 1.

Half double crochet (hdc) in back bar of first stitch (st).

Half double crochet (hdc) in back bar of each stitch (st) across row.

Turn work.

(42 half double crochet {hdc})

Row 3: Repeat (rep) row 2.

Fasten off.

Body

Row 1 (wrong side {WS}): Join seafoam in back bar of first stitch (st).

Half double crochet (hdc) in back bar of first stitch (st) (this is the same stitch {st} you pulled the new loop {lp} of yarn through).

Half double crochet (hdc) in back bar of next 2 stitches (sts).

> *Working 2 stitches (sts) in the same stitch (st) increases your stitch (st) count by 1 stitch (st).*

*2 half double crochet (hdc) in back bar of next stitch (st).

Half double crochet (hdc) in back bar of next 4 stitches (sts).

Repeat (rep) from * to last 4 stitches (sts).

2 half double crochet (hdc) in back bar of next stitch (st).

Half double crochet (hdc) in back bar of last 3 stitches (sts).

Turn work.

> *On the last row you crocheted 2 stitches (sts) in a single stitch (st) a total of 8 times so you now have 50 half double crochet (hdc) stitches (sts) on your row.*

(50 half double crochet {hdc})

Row 2 (right side {RS}): Chain (ch) 1.

Half double crochet (hdc) in back bar of first stitch (st).

Half double crochet (hdc) in back bar of next stitch (st).

*Half double crochet (hdc) in back loop (lp) of next 2 stitches (sts).

Half double crochet (hdc) in back bar of next 2 stitches (sts).

Repeat (rep) from * across row.

Turn work.

(50 half double crochet {hdc})

Row 3: Chain (ch) 1.

Half double crochet (hdc) in back loop (lp) of first stitch (st).

Half double crochet (hdc) in back loop (lp) of next stitch (st).

*Half double crochet (hdc) in back bar of next 2 stitches (sts).

Half double crochet (hdc) in back loop (lp) of next 2 stitches (sts).

Repeat (rep) from * across row.

Turn work.

(50 half double crochet {hdc})

Repeat (rep) rows 2 and 3 until piece is about 68 inches long measuring from foundation chain (ch) to last row ending with row 3.

Fasten off at end of last row.

Contrasting Stripe

With teal, repeat (rep) Contrasting Stripe rows 1–3.

Scarf End

With off white, repeat (rep) Body rows 1–3.

Repeat (rep) Body rows 2 and 3 until end is same length as beginning (beg) ending with row 2.

Fasten off at end of last row.

Weave in all yarn ends.

Pompoms

Make 2 pompoms in each of the 3 colors with a finished pompom size of around 1⅝ inches leaving a long tying strand.

For each side of scarf
Bunch one of each color pompom together *(tog)*.

Tie pompoms in place.

Weave in yarn ends.

Optional Removable Pompoms

Attach shank button to pompoms with tying strands, weave yarn ends into pompoms.

Using spaces *(sps)* between half double crochet *(hdc)* for buttonholes, button pompoms in desired location on 2nd Contrasting Stripe row. ●

Part Seven

DOUBLE CROCHET (ABBREVIATED DC)

Double crochet is a taller stitch than half double crochet.

How to Make a Double Crochet in a Chain Stitch

Step 1: Yarn over the hook from back to front, skip the first 3 back bar of chains from the hook, then insert the hook in the 4th chain.

Note: You can work through different portions of the chain stitch, but in this book we are working into the back bar of the chains.

Remember not to count the loop on the hook as a chain and to always bring the loops up onto the working portion of the hook as this is what sizes your stitches.

Step 2: Yarn over the hook from back to front and draw it through the chain stitch *(3 loops on hook)*.

Step 3: Yarn over the hook from back to front and draw through the first 2 loops on the hook *(2 loops on hook)*.

Step 4: Yarn over the hook from back to front and draw through both loops on the hook.

You have now completed one double crochet; one loop remains on the hook.

For the next stitch, yarn over the hook from back to front and go into the next back bar of chain, then repeat steps 2 through 4. Repeat in each remaining chain across. Remember when counting the first 3 chain stitches you skipped at the beginning of the row count as one double crochet.

After you turn your work, make 3 chains and you are ready to start the next row. The chains made before beginning the next row count as a stitch *(unless your pattern specifies otherwise)*. This is called the turning chain and is made so that the yarn is at the right height to make the first double crochet stitch on the next row.

Learn to Crochet: A Beginner's Guide

How to Make a Double Crochet in a Stitch

Skip the first stitch of the previous row since the turning chain counts as a stitch.

Step 1: Yarn over the hook from back to front and insert the hook under the top 2 loops of the next stitch.

Step 2: Yarn over the hook from back to front, then draw it through the stitch.

Step 3: Yarn over the hook from back to front, then draw it through 2 loops on the hook twice.

You will work double crochet in this manner across all stitches.

You will count the chain-3 at the start as a stitch when counting stitches for the row.

Loops Used in Double Crochet

Just like single crochet, when following a pattern, it is always assumed that the double crochet stitch will be worked by inserting the hook under the top 2 loops of the stitch unless the pattern specifically says to double crochet only in the front loop or double crochet only in the back loop.

Back Loop

Front Loop

HOW TO CHANGE COLOR IN THE LAST TWO LOOPS OF A STITCH

To work a color change to the last 2 loops of a stitch, you will work the stitch until 2 loops remain on the hook. The photo below shows a double crochet as an example. But any crochet stitch can work a color change in this manner.

Then drop the old yarn color *(cutting if directed to do so in the pattern)*, pull the new yarn color through the 2 loops, leaving a tail about 5 inches long to weave in later.

This completes the color change. Work the next stitches with the new color and weave in yarn tails when work is complete or after a couple of rows of stitching.

How to Change Color on a Chain

After you make your last chain with the first color, cut the yarn, leaving a 5-inch strand. Pull the loop on the hook up till the end of the strand pops through the last chain.

Insert the hook under the back loop of the last chain where the yarn strand was drawn through.

With the next color, pull the yarn through the chain, leaving a 5-inch beginning strand.

Then continue making chains as normal. ●

Twisted Knot Ear Cozy

This is a fun-to-stitch little ear warmer with a twist. You will want to stitch one for all your friends.

Finished Measurements
22 inches wide x 5 inches high before joining

Materials
- At least 200 yds of smooth worsted-weight acrylic/wool yarn in 1 color for solid version or in 2 different colors for two color version
- Plymouth Yarn Encore Worsted medium (worsted) weight acrylic/wool yarn (3½ oz/200 yds/100g per skein):
  - 1 skein #1232 light greenhouse
- Plymouth Yarn Encore Colorspun medium (worsted) weight acrylic/wool yarn (3½ oz/200 yds/100g per skein):
  - 1 skein #7990 raspberry drift

Supplies in Project Bag
- Size 5mm crochet hook (which can also be listed as size H or 8)
- Tapestry needle
- Scissors
- Tape measure
- Locking stitch markers

Gauge
15 stitches (sts) = 5 inches; 16 rows = 5 inches

Pattern Notes
The ear cozy is created by working a rectangle from the bottom edge to the top edge.

The short ends are then folded over each other and sewn together for the knotted look.

You can make this in 1 solid color or in 2 colors depending on your preference.

Chain-1 at beginning of a row does not count as a stitch. It builds up the height of the row.

Skills Needed
- Make a loose foundation chain.
- Identify parts of a chain.
- Weave in yarn ends.
- Single crochet.
- Join pieces with whipstitch.
- Crochet in back loop.
- Understand gauge.
- Change color in a chain.
- Double crochet.
- Change color in a stitch.
- Identify back bar of chain.

EAR COZY
Row 1 (right side {RS}): With color of choice,

make 68 chains (chs).

Turn to work back across foundation chain (ch).

Skip (sk) first chain (ch) closest to hook.

Single crochet (sc) in back bar of next chain (ch) (see page 9).

Single crochet (sc) in back bar of each chain (ch) across.

Turn work.

(67 single crochet {sc})

Row 2: Chain (ch) 1 (see Pattern Notes).

Single crochet (sc) in both loops (lps) of first stitch (st).

> *Gauge is the number of stitches (sts) the designer worked over a specific measurement. To achieve the finished measurements of a pattern, you will need to match these numbers. 15 stitches (sts) is what the designer worked over 5 inches using the given yarn and hook in the Materials list. And she achieved 16 rows of stitching over 5 inches. You may need a smaller or larger hook to get the same numbers.*

Note: Brackets are used much like * in the previous pattern. You repeat the instructions inside the brackets over and over again the number of times stated or for as long as stated.

[Double crochet (dc) in **back loop (lp)** (see page 38) only of next stitch (st).

Single crochet (sc) in both loops (lps) of next stitch (st)] across to end of row.

Turn work.

(34 single crochet {sc}, 33 double crochet {dc})

Row 3: Chain (ch) 1.

Single crochet (sc) in both loops (lps) of first stitch (st).

Single crochet (sc) in back loop (lp) only of each stitch (st) across to last stitch (st).

Single crochet (sc) in both loops (lps) of last stitch (st).

Turn work.

(67 single crochet {sc})

Repeat (rep) rows 2 and 3 until piece is about 5 inches high measuring from foundation chain (ch) to last row ending with row 2.

Fasten off at end of last row, leaving a 15-inch tail for joining.

Remove all stitch markers.

Finishing

Place ear cozy on table with wrong side (WS) touching table and long edges parallel to you.

Place a stitch marker in end of row on left side about halfway up side.

Bring bottom right corner to stitch marker and pin in place with same stitch marker.

DID YOU KNOW?
In the United States, the stitch names single crochet and double crochet refer to how many times the yarn is drawn through the loops on the hook after the yarn has been drawn through the stitch. To make a single crochet, after the yarn is drawn through the stitch, you place the yarn over the hook then draw the yarn through 2 loops on the hook a single time. To make a double crochet, after the yarn is drawn through the stitch, you place the yarn over the hook then draw the yarn through 2 loops on the hook twice or double the number of times!

Twisted Knot Ear Cozy

Fold unpinned top right corner around to the back of the ear cozy to the stitch marker, encasing top left corner and side.

Then fold bottom left side around to the back to the folded edge and hold in place.

You should now have 4 layers.

Remove stitch marker.

With tapestry needle and 15-inch ending yarn tail, **whipstitch** *(see page 19)* across row ends working through all 4 layers.

Weave in all yarn ends.

Turn Ear Cozy so right side *(RS)* is showing.

> *Remember to leave 5-inch tails when fastening off and joining new yarn.*

SIZING & ADJUSTMENTS

Measure to see if first row is same size as circumference of your head. Cozy should have 0–1 inch of negative ease.

If it is too small, you can redo row 1 adding an even number of beginning *(beg)* chains *(chs)* to each color.

For instance, the pattern says to chain *(ch)* 34 with each color so you could chain *(ch)* 36 with each color to begin *(beg)*.

If it is too big, you can redo row 1 subtracting an even number of beginning *(beg)* chain *(chs)* from each color.

For instance, you could chain *(ch)* 32 with each color to begin *(beg)*.

Bonus Project: Twisted Knot Ear Cozy: Two Colors

TWO-COLOR EAR COZY

Row 1 (right side {RS}): With light greenhouse,

make 34 chains *(chs)*.

Fasten off.

Pull loop *(lp)* on hook up until end of strand pops through last chain *(ch)* *(see page 39).*

Insert hook under **back loop *(lp)*** *(see page 39)* of last chain *(ch)* where yarn strand was drawn through.

With raspberry drift,

yarn over *(yo)* hook.

Draw yarn through chain *(ch)*,

make 34 chains *(chs)*.

Turn to work back across foundation chain *(ch)*.

Skip *(sk)* first chain *(ch)* closest to hook.

Single crochet *(sc)* in back bar of next chain *(ch)* *(see page 9).*

Single crochet *(sc)* in back bar of each raspberry drift chain *(ch)* across to last chain *(ch)* of this color.

Change color *(see page 39)* by inserting hook in back bar of last raspberry drift chain *(ch)*.

Yarn over *(yo)* hook.

Draw yarn through chain *(ch)* (2 loops {lps} on hook).

Drop raspberry drift strand to front of work *(right side {RS})*.

With light greenhouse,

Yarn over *(yo)* hook.

Leaving a 5-inch beginning (beg) strand in back of work,

draw yarn through both loops (lps) on hook.

Move raspberry drift strand under light greenhouse strand to back of your work (wrong side {WS}).

With light greenhouse,

single crochet (sc) in back bar of each light greenhouse chain (ch) across.

Turn work.

(34 light greenhouse single crochet {sc}, 33 raspberry drift single crochet {sc})

Row 2: Chain (ch) 1 (see Pattern Notes).

Single crochet (sc) in both loops (lps) of first stitch (st).

[Double crochet (dc) in **back loop (lp)** (see page 38) only of next stitch (st).

Single crochet (sc) in both loops (lps) of next stitch (st)] across to last greenhouse stitch (st).

Change color by working a single crochet (sc) in back loop (lp) of last raspberry drift stitch (st) until you have 2 loops (lps) left on hook.

Drop greenhouse strand to back of work (right side {RS}).

Pick up raspberry drift strand which is in front of work.

Yarn over (yo) hook.

Draw yarn through 2 loops (lps) on your hook completing stitch (st).

Move greenhouse strand under raspberry drift strand to front of your work (wrong side {WS}).

With raspberry drift, single crochet (sc) in both loops (lps) of next stitch (st).

Repeat (rep) between [ ] across.

Turn work.

> *Brackets are used much like * in the previous pattern. You repeat the instructions inside the brackets over and over again the number of times stated or for as long as stated.*

> *This means you will go back to the bracketed instructions and work them over and over again until the end of the row.*

(34 single crochet {sc}, 33 double crochet {dc})

Row 3: Chain (ch) 1.

Single crochet (sc) in both loops (lps) of first stitch (st).

Single crochet (sc) in back loop (lp) only of each stitch (st) across to last raspberry drift stitch (st).

Change color by working a single crochet (sc) in back loop (lp) of last raspberry drift stitch (st) until you have 2 loops (lps) left on hook.

Drop raspberry drift strand to front of work (right side {RS}).

Pick up greenhouse strand which is in back of work.

Yarn over (yo) hook.

Draw yarn through 2 loops (lps) on your hook completing stitch (st).

Move raspberry drift strand under greenhouse strand to back of your work (wrong side {WS}).

With greenhouse, single crochet (sc) in back loop (lp) of each stitch (st) across to last stitch (st).

Single crochet (sc) in both loops (lps) of last stitch (st).

Turn work.

(67 single crochet {sc})

Repeat (rep) rows 2 and 3 until piece is about 5 inches high measuring from foundation chain (ch) to last row ending with row 2.

Fasten off raspberry drift at end of last row, leaving a 15-inch strand for joining.

Fasten off greenhouse at end of last row, leaving a 5-inch strand.

Remove all stitch markers.

Finishing

Follow finishing instructions for previous Ear Cozy pattern.

Weave in all yarn ends. ●

> *Refer to sidebar for sizing and adjustment tips.*

Part Eight

ROUND & ROUND WE GO

There are several ways to begin crocheting in rounds. Each of the next couple of projects in this book will introduce a new method. We will start with joining a chain.

HOW TO JOIN A CHAIN TO FORM A RING

There are actually 2 methods to join a chain to form a ring. Once you have learned both, you can choose which method you prefer and interchange them in a pattern.

Step 1. Make a given number of chain stitches, then, being careful not to twist the chain, make a stitch in the first chain to form a ring. After the ring is made, you work in the foundation chain stitches the same as you would when working in back and forth rows.

Note: Your beginning number of chain stitches is the same as the number of stitches you will be working on your round. The downside to this method is that if the chain stitches accidently get twisted, you end up with an infinity loop instead of a ring.

Step 2. The second option is to treat the first round like a row and place the required stitches into the foundation chain before making a stitch in the first stitch to form a ring.

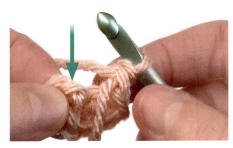

This method works better for most as a row of stitches is less likely to get twisted.

Note: In this method, since your first stitch will be worked into the 2nd chain from the hook as if it were a row, you will need 1 more beginning foundation chain stitch than the required number of stitches on your first round. The downside to this method is that you will need to sew the bottom of the first and last foundation chain together with the beginning strand to complete your project.

How to Slip Stitch

Step 1: Insert the hook in the indicated chain or stitch.

Step 2: Yarn over the hook.

Step 3: Draw the yarn through the chain or stitch and also through the loop on the hook.

It is best to make slip stitches in a calm, relaxed atmosphere. Not only does the beginning chain of all projects need to be worked loosely, the slip stitches will need to be worked loosely as well. Slip stitches take a little patience and practice, but after working a few rows, they will become much more manageable.

Which Loops to Use

Unlike single crochet stitches where it is standard to single crochet under both loops unless the pattern states otherwise, slip stitches have no such standard. Therefore, it is important to check the pattern for placement before crocheting a slip stitch.

HOW TO CROCHET IN A RING

You can also start crocheting in the round by placing your stitches inside a chain ring. This is helpful if starting with a small chain of 3 or 4 stitches.

After you have made your chain stitches, join them into a ring by making a slip stitch in the first chain you made. Try not to twist the chain stitches, but if they twist, it won't matter for this method.

Make the first round of stitches by inserting the hook inside the center of the ring instead of in the chain stitches.

After a few rounds have been worked, you can pull the beginning strand gently to close any gap that was created when working your stitches or you can leave a small opening in the center of your work to create a different look.

HOW TO FIND THE END OF A ROUND

Since there is no edge on a round, you have 2 options:

Step 1. Count every stitch on every round so that you know when you are at the end of a round. The downside to this method is that it takes total concentration, so you don't lose your count. Some people count out loud so others in the room know not to disturb them.

Step 2. Put a stitch marker in the first stitch on the round so that you will know when you have reached the end of the round. Then move the stitch marker up every round to mark the beginning of each new round. This is a much safer method, the only downside being that it takes a little more time to move the marker up each round.

HOW TO END A ROUND WITH AN INVISIBLE JOIN

Unlike rows where you just cut your yarn and pull the loop on your hook up until the end of the strand pops through, rounds require a few additional steps for a smooth edge..

Step 1. After you work your last stitch on your last round, slip stitch in both loops of the next 2 stitches.

Then cut the yarn, leaving a 7-inch strand. Gently, so as not to tighten the last slip stitch, pull the loop on the hook up until the end of the strand pops through.

Step 2. Skip the next stitch on the round. With your hook in back of your work, insert your hook going from the back of your piece to the front of your piece through both horizontal top loops of the next stitch.

Yarn over the hook with the 7-inch strand and draw the strand through the stitch. The ending strand is now in the back of your work.

Step 3. Go back to the slip stitch where the cut yarn popped through. With your hook in the back of your work, insert the hook going in from the bottom and out through the top of the back loop of the slip stitch.

Yarn over the hook with the 7-inch strand and draw the strand down through the back loop.

Step 4. Gently adjust the stitch just made with the 7-inch strand so that no join can be seen and your last round appears to have continuous circling horizontal V shapes. Weave in the ending yarn strand.

HOW TO JOIN A NEW COLOR ON A ROUND

After you have ended the round with the previous color, insert your hook under the top 2 loops of the stitch where the new color is to be joined.

With the new color, leaving a 5-inch strand at the beginning, yarn over the hook, draw the yarn through the stitch.

Then chain 1. The chain-1 will join your yarn and will also count as the beginning chain-1 to build up the height of your row. ●

Learn to Crochet: A Beginner's Guide

Part Eight 47

Pompom Tips Cap

Master working in the round by creating a hat with no shaping and cute little pompoms to jazz it up.

> *The finished cap will fit a head circumference of 20–22 inches. This type of cap typically has 1–3 inches of negative ease, meaning the finished cap circumference is smaller than the wearer's head circumference.*

Finished Measurements
19 inches in circumference x 8½ inches high

Materials
- At least 170 yds of smooth worsted-weight acrylic yarn for cap and at least 150 yds for brim
- Lion Brand Yarn Vanna's Choice Solid medium (worsted) weight acrylic/rayon yarn (3½ oz/170 yds/100g per skein):
    1 skein each #146I dusty purple and #101A pink

Supplies in Project Bag
- Size 5mm crochet hook (which can also be listed as size H or 8)
- Tapestry needle
- Scissors
- Tape measure
- Locking stitch markers

Additional Items
- 22mm round shank buttons: 2
- 24 inches of round cord elastic—light stretch

Gauge
12 stitches (sts) = 4 inches; 13 rounds (rnds) = 4 inches

Pattern Notes
Hat is worked from the top down in a tube that is created by working in continuous rounds or a spiral. Pompoms are made and attached in a way to make them easily removable. This is achieved by always working the first stitch of each round directly in the top of the first stitch of the previous round. You will use a marker to help identify stitches and move the marker up as you progress.

The first round is then sewn together to close it off with pompoms added in each tip.

Skills Needed
- Make a loose foundation chain.
- Identify parts of a chain.
- Weave in yarn ends.
- Single crochet.
- Crochet in back loop.
- Slip stitch.
- Make a pompom.
- Join a chain to form a ring.
- Mark or count a round.
- Invisible join.
- Join a new color in a round.
- Identify back bar of chain.

CAP
Top
Round (rnd) 1 (right side {RS}): With cap color of choice, make 57 chains (chs).

Leave a 7-inch beginning (beg) yarn tail for joining foundation chain (ch).

Turn to work back across foundation chain (ch).

Skip (sk) first chain (ch) closest to hook.

Single crochet (sc) in back bar of next chain (ch) *(see page 9).*

Place stitch marker in stitch (st) just made to mark beginning (beg) stitch (st) of round (rnd).

> *Gauge is the number of stitches (sts) the designer worked over a specific measurement. To achieve the finished measurements of a pattern, you will need to match these numbers. 12 stitches (sts) is what the designer worked over 4 inches using the given yarn and hook in the Materials list. And she achieved 13 rounds of stitching over 4 inches. You may need a smaller or larger hook to get the same numbers.*

Single crochet (sc) in back bar of each chain (ch) across.

Do not turn.

(56 single crochet {sc})

Round (rnd) 2: Be careful not to twist stitches (sts).

Single crochet (sc) in marked stitch (st) on round (rnd) 1 forming a ring of stitches (sts).

Move stitch marker to stitch (st) just made.

Single crochet (sc) in each stitch (st) around.

(56 single crochet {sc})

Round (rnd) 3: Single crochet (sc) in marked stitch (st).

Move stitch marker to stitch (st) just made.

Single crochet (sc) in each stitch (st) around.

(56 single crochet {sc})

Repeat (rep) round (rnd) 3 until piece is about 7 inches long, measuring from foundation chain (ch) to last round (rnd).

After last stitch (st) is completed, join last round (rnd) with **invisible join (inv join)** (see page 46).

Brim

Round (rnd) 1 (right side {RS}): Join brim color of choice in back loop (lp) (see page 20) **of any stitch (st) on last round (rnd) of Cap.**

Single crochet (sc) in same back loop (lp) as joining.

Place stitch marker in stitch (st) just made.

Single crochet (sc) in back loop (lp) of each stitch (st) around.

(56 single crochet {sc})

Round (rnd) 2: Working in both loops (lps),

single crochet (sc) in marked stitch (st).

Move stitch marker to stitch (st) just made.

Single crochet (sc) in each stitch (st) around.

(56 single crochet {sc})

Repeat (rep) round (rnd) 2 for 3 more rounds (rnds) making Brim a total of 5 rounds (rnds) high.

After last stitch (st) is completed, join last round (rnd) with invisible join (inv join).

Remove all stitch markers.

Finishing

With tapestry needle and beginning (beg) 7-inch yarn tail, sew bottom of first and last foundation chain (ch) together (tog) then weave in end.

BONUS PROJECT: Ye Olde Owl Cap

Turn your Pompom Tips Cap into a Ye Olde Owl Cap by adding owl features and omitting the pompoms.

Cut 30-inch strand of cap color yarn.

With right side *(RS)* showing, place cap on table then flatten the beginning *(beg)* foundation chain *(ch)* so that the first 28 chains *(chs)* are touching the last 28 chains *(chs)*.

With tapestry needle and 30-inch strand, using **invisible seam** *(see page 20)*, leaving a 7-inch strand at beginning *(beg)* to attach a button, sew across foundation chains *(chs)* at top of cap, end of 30-inch strand will also be used to attach a button.

With tapestry needle, using beginning *(beg)* and ending yarn strands, sew a button inside cap, on the invisible seam, 2 or 3 stitches *(sts)* from each corner so that edge of button is at top corner of cap.

Weave in ends.

Pompom
Make 2.

Cut a 12-inch length of elastic.

Make a Brim color pompom around 1⅝ inches leaving long tying strands.

With tying strands, tie center of elastic to pompom.

Trim tying strands.

Tie the 2 ends of the elastic into a sturdy knot creating a ½-inch button loop *(lp)*.

Trim elastic ends.

Using hook, draw elastic button loop *(lp)* through a stitch *(st)* on front of cap as close to button as possible.

Attach button loop *(lp)* to button.

Additional Skills Needed
- Make French knots.
- Whipstitch pieces on top of pieces.
- Half double crochet.
- Increase.
- Double crochet.
- Crochet in a ring.

Materials
- At least 50 yds each of 3 different colors, plus the leftover yarn from making the Pompom Tips Cap
- Lion Brand Yarn Vanna's Choice medium (worsted) weight acrylic/rayon yarn (3½ oz/170 yds/100g per skein):
  - 1 skein each #134A terracotta (top of cap) and #099H linen (brim)
  - Small amounts #100 white (eyes), #146I dusty purple (inner eyes) and #158I mustard (nose)

Additional Items
1 Finished Pompom Tips Cap without the pompoms

Nose
Row 1 (right side {RS}):

With mustard,

make 7 chains *(chs)*.

Turn to work back across foundation chain *(ch)*.

Skip *(sk)* first chain *(ch)* closest to hook.

Double crochet *(dc)* in back bar of next chain *(ch)* *(see page 37)*.

Working in back bar of each chain *(ch)* across,

double crochet *(dc)* in next chain *(ch)*.

Half double crochet *(hdc)* in next chain *(ch)*.

Single crochet *(sc)* in next 2 chains *(chs)*.

Slip stitch *(sl st)* in last chain *(ch)*.

Fasten off leaving a 10-inch tail for sewing.

(2 double crochet {dc}, 1 half double crochet {hdc}, 2 single crochet {sc}, 1 slip stitch {sl st})

Weave in beginning *(beg)* yarn end.

With tapestry needle and ending yarn tail, using photo for placement guide, whipstitch nose to cap.

Weave in end.

Eye
Make 2.

Round (rnd) 1 (right side {RS}):

With dusty purple,

make 3 chains *(chs)*.

Slip stitch *(sl st)* *(see page 45)* in first chain *(ch)* made forming a ring.

Single crochet *(sc)* in the ring.

Place a stitch marker in the single crochet *(sc)* just made to mark beginning *(beg)* of round *(rnd)*.

Work 5 more single crochet *(sc)* in ring creating a ring of stitches *(sts)*.

(6 single crochet {sc})

Round (rnd) 2: Single crochet *(sc)* in marked stitch *(st)*.

Move stitch marker to stitch *(st)* just made.

Single crochet *(sc)* in same stitch *(st)* as last stitch *(st)*.

2 single crochet *(sc)* in each stitch *(st)* around.

Remove stitch marker.

Join round *(rnd)* with **invisible join (inv join)** *(see page 46)*.

(12 single crochet {sc})

Pull beginning *(beg)* tail gently to close opening then weave in end.

Round (rnd) 3 *(right side {RS})*:

Join white in any stitch *(st)* on last round *(rnd)*.

> By working 2 stitches (sts) into the same stitch (st), you are creating increases (inc)—additional stitches (sts) in the round (rnd)—so that it lays flat.

Single crochet (sc) in same stitch (st) as joining.

Place stitch marker in stitch (st) just made.

2 single crochet (sc) in next stitch (st).

[Single crochet (sc) in next stitch (st).

2 single crochet (sc) in next stitch (st)] 5 more times.

(18 single crochet {sc})

Round (rnd) 4: Single crochet (sc) in first stitch (st).

Move stitch marker to stitch (st) just made.

(Chain {ch} 3, single crochet {sc}) in single crochet {sc} just made.

Chain (ch) 3.

Single crochet (sc) in next st.

Chain (ch) 3.

Single crochet (sc) in next st.

Chain (ch) 3.

[(Single crochet {sc}, chain {ch} 3, single crochet {sc}) in next stitch {st}.

Chain (ch) 3.

Single crochet (sc) in next stitch (st).

Chain (ch) 3.

Single crochet (sc) in next stitch (st).

Chain (ch) 3] 5 times.

Slip stitch (sl st) in both loops (lps) of first stitch (st) to join round (rnd).

Remove stitch marker.

Fasten off, leaving 15-inch tail for sewing.

(24 single crochet {sc}, 24 chain-3 spaces {ch-3 sps})

Weave in beginning (beg) end.

With tapestry needle and ending tail, using photo for placement guide, whipstitch eye on cap through stitches (sts) on round (rnd) 3.

Weave in end.

Instructions in parentheses are worked in the single indicated stitch (st) and all the instructions within the square brackets are worked the indicated number of times.

For Each Ear

Cut 4 strands of brim color each 9 inches long.

Turn cap so wrong side (WS) is showing.

Draw 4½ inches of all 4 strands through a corner stitch (st) at seam.

Tie overhand knot in center of strands attaching them to the stitch (st) and creating 4 yarn ends on each side of the knot.

Turn cap so right side (RS) is showing.

With hook, draw 4 yarn ends through stitch (st) at seam.

Draw remaining (rem) 4 yarn ends through stitch (st) 1 stitch (st) below corner seam.

Cut 2 10-inch strands of cap color yarn.

Scrunch each corner of cap together (tog) to form ear shape.

Tie 1 strand around each corner to hold ear in place.

French Knots

With tapestry needle and a long strand of cap color yarn, randomly embroider **French knots** *(see illustration)* on front of brim wrapping yarn around needle 3 times to form the knots. ●

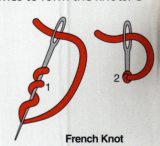

French Knot

DID YOU KNOW?
YouTube celebrity Summer Bjarnarson of Summer's Tips and Stitches suggests sewing a button in the top of a child's cap, then attaching the pompom via an elastic to the button. Attaching the pompom in this fashion allows the pompom to be removed before washing the cap. She ought to know—she makes a cap for each student in her 2nd grade class every year!

PART EIGHT

Part 9

HOW TO CROCHET IN THE ROUND USING BOTH SIDES OF A CHAIN

To make a round of stitches in an oval shape instead of a circle, you can make a chain then work your stitches on both sides of the chain, creating an elongated center.

Remember, a chain stitch has a front loop, back loop and back bar.

Once you have worked stitches in the back bar of each chain across the foundation chain, you can turn the foundation chain 180 degrees and work stitches back across the foundation chain through the front and back loops of the chains.

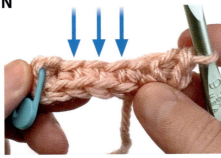

To make the turn smoothly, the pattern will instruct you to crochet more than one stitch in the first and last foundation chain, causing the stitches to curve around to the other side of the chain.

HOW TO CROCHET TWO PIECES TOGETHER

In addition to sewing pieces together, pieces can also be joined by crocheting them together. Holding one crocheted piece behind another, you can insert your hook through both layers to make stitches that join the 2 pieces together. ●

DID YOU KNOW?
Even though a crochet hook was used to make the stitches, the oldest known crochet stitch was called shepherd's knitting. Today we call shepherd's knitting … slip stitch!

Window Panes Bag

Color peeks out through the mesh in this fun little project bag that has you practicing a lot of your crochet skills.

Finished Measurements
26 inches in circumference x 10 inches tall

Materials
- At least 300 yds of smooth worsted-weight cotton yarn in 2 different colors
- Premier Yarns Cotton Sprout Solid medium (worsted) weight cotton yarn (3½ oz/180 yds/100g per skein):
  - 2 skeins each #29 white and #18 blue

Supplies in Project Bag
- Size 5mm crochet hook (which can also be listed as size H or 8)
- Tapestry needle
- Scissors
- Tape measure
- Locking stitch markers in 2 different colors

Additional Item
- 1 sheet ultra stiff 7-mesh plastic canvas (optional)

Gauge
13 stitches (sts) = 4 inches;
15 rounds (rnds) = 4 inches

Pattern Notes
Bag Liner is worked from the bottom up in spiral rounds, meaning the first and last stitches of each round are not joined. The first stitch of each round is worked directly in the first stitch of the previous round, without joining the rounds.

Increases are made to shape first the bottom and then the sides are worked.

You will work the liner of the bag and then go back and work the outer mesh portion of the bag.

The Outer Bag is worked in joined rounds.

Little loop straps are made and attached at 4 points and then twisted rope ties are created and run through the loops for a fun closure to the bag.

Join new yarn with a slip stitch unless otherwise instructed.

Stitch markers are moved up each round as work progresses.

Chain-1 at beginning of round or row doesn't count as a stitch. It builds up the height of the round or row.

Chain-5 at beginning of a round counts as first double crochet and chain-2 space.

Skills Needed
- Make a loose foundation chain.
- Identify parts of a chain.
- Weave in yarn ends.
- Single crochet.
- Sew whipstitch.
- Sew running stitch.
- Single crochet in a chain space.
- Slip stitch.
- Tie overhand knot.
- Half double crochet.
- Identify 3 horizontal loops of half double crochet.
- Increase.
- Double crochet.
- Mark or count a round.
- Invisible join.
- Join a new color in a round.
- Crochet both sides of chain.
- Crochet pieces together.

BAG
Bottom
Round (rnd) 1 (right side {RS}): With white, make 3 chains *(chs)*.

Gauge is the number of stitches (sts) the designer worked over a specific measurement. To achieve the finished measurements of a pattern, you will need to match these numbers. 13 stitches (sts) is what the designer worked over 4 inches using the given yarn and hook in the Materials list. And she achieved 15 rounds of stitching over 4 inches. You may need a smaller or larger hook to get the same numbers.

Place a first color **stitch marker** (see Pattern Notes) through **front** and **back loop** (lp) (see page 6) of 2nd chain (ch) made.

Make 18 more chains (chs).

Turn to work back across foundation chain (ch).

Skip (sk) first chain (ch) closest to hook.

Single crochet (sc) in back bar of next chain (ch) (see page 9).

Place a first color stitch marker in stitch (st) just made to mark beginning (beg) of round (rnd).

2 single crochet (sc) in same chain (ch) as last stitch (st) was worked to shape side of bag.

Single crochet (sc) in back bar of next 17 chains (chs) for back of bag.

Without moving marker,

single crochet (sc) in back bar of chain (ch) where front and back loop (lp) of chain (ch) are marked.

Single crochet (sc) in back bar of last chain (ch).

Place a 2nd color stitch marker in stitch (st) just made to mark beginning (beg) of 2nd side of bag.

2 single crochet (sc) in same chain (ch) as last stitch (st) was worked to shape side of bag.

Turn to work across bottom of foundation chain (ch).

Working in both front and back loop (lp) of each foundation chain (ch) across,

single crochet (sc) in marked chain (ch).

Remove stitch marker.

Single crochet (sc) in remaining (rem) 17 chains (chs) across.

(42 single crochet {sc})

Round (rnd) 2: *Single crochet (sc) in marked stitch (st).

Move marker to stitch (st) just made.

Single crochet (sc) in same stitch (st) as last stitch (st) worked.

2 single crochet (sc) in next 2 stitches (sts) to shape side of bag.

Single crochet (sc) in next 18 stitches (sts) to next marked stitch (st).

Repeat (rep) all of round (rnd) 2 instructions from * to beginning-of-round (beg-of-rnd) first color stitch marker.

(48 single crochet {sc})

Round (rnd) 3: *Single crochet (sc) in marked stitch (st).

Move marker to stitch (st) just made.

Single crochet (sc) in same stitch (st) as last stitch (st) worked.

2 single crochet (sc) in next 5 stitches (sts) to shape side of bag.

Single crochet (sc) in next 18 stitches (sts) to next marked stitch (st).

Repeat (rep) all of round (rnd) 3 instructions from * to beginning-of-round (beg-of-rnd) first color stitch marker.

(60 single crochet {sc})

Round (rnd) 4: *Single crochet (sc) in marked stitch (st).

Move marker to stitch (st) just made.

Single crochet (sc) in each stitch (st) to next marked stitch (st).

Repeat (rep) all of round (rnd) 4 instructions from * to beginning-of-round (beg-of-rnd) first color stitch marker.

(60 single crochet {sc})

> *The instructions between the braces are repeated the number of times indicated, then all the instructions between the square brackets are repeated (rep) the number of time indicated. Then, continue with the instructions for completing the round.*

Round (rnd) 5: *Single crochet (sc) in marked stitch (st).

Move marker to stitch (st) just made.

[{2 single crochet (sc) in next stitch (st).

Single crochet (sc) in next stitch (st)} twice.

2 single crochet (sc) in next stitch (st)] 5 times.

Single crochet (sc) in next 19 stitches (sts) to next marked stitch (st).

Repeat (rep) all of round (rnd) 5 instructions from * to beginning-of-round (beg-of-rnd) first color stitch marker.

(72 single crochet {sc})

Round (rnd) 6: Repeat (rep) round (rnd) 4. (72 single crochet {sc})

Round (rnd) 7: *Single crochet (sc) in marked stitch (st).

Move marker to stitch (st) just made.

Single crochet (sc) in next 3 stitches (sts).

[2 single crochet (sc) in next 3 stitches (sts).

Single crochet (sc) in next 4 stitches (sts)] twice.

Single crochet (sc) in next 18 stitches (sts) to next marked stitch (st).

Repeat (rep) all of round (rnd) 7 instructions from * to beginning-of-round (beg-of-rnd) first color stitch marker.

(84 single crochet {sc})

Keep first color stitch marker marking beginning (beg) of round (rnd) and continue moving it up with each round (rnd).

Remove 2nd color stitch marker marking beginning (beg) of 2nd side of bag.

Outer Bag

Round (rnd) 1: Continuing with white, single crochet (sc) in each stitch (st) around. (84 single crochet {sc})

Rounds (rnds) 2–5: [Repeat (rep) round (rnd) 1] 4 times.

Round (rnd) 6: Half double crochet (hdc) in each stitch (st) around. (84 half double crochet {hdc})

Drop loop (lp) from hook, place a first color stitch marker in dropped loop (lp) to keep it from unraveling. Do not cut yarn.

Bag Liner

Round (rnd) 1 (wrong side {WS}): Turn bag so that wrong side (WS) is facing.

Join blue *(see page 47)* in **back bar of half double crochet (hdc)** *(see page 32)* where first color stitch marker is, do not move marker.

Single crochet (sc) in same back bar as joining.

Place a 2nd color stitch marker in stitch (st) just made to mark beginning (beg) of liner rounds (rnds).

Move marked bag color loop (lp) and yarn strand to back of work which is right side (RS) of work.

Single crochet (sc) in back bar of each half double crochet (hdc) around. (84 single crochet {sc})

Round (rnd) 2: Single crochet (sc) in each stitch (st) around. (84 single crochet {sc})

Repeat (rep) round (rnd) 2 until Bag Liner is about 7 inches long, measuring from first liner round (rnd) to last round (rnd).

Single crochet (sc) on round (rnd) 1 will push front and back loop (lp) of half double crochet (hdc) to back of work which is right side (RS) of bag.

Window Panes Bag

Drop loop *(lp)* from hook, place a 2nd color stitch marker in dropped loop *(lp)* to keep it from unraveling. Do not cut yarn.

Outer Bag Panes

Round (rnd) 1 (right side {RS}): Turn bag so that right side *(RS)* is facing, remove first color marker from dropped bag loop *(lp)* then place loop *(lp)* on hook.

With white, slip stitch *(sl st)* in the marked first half double crochet *(hdc)*.

Move marker to stitch *(st)* just made to mark beginning *(beg)* of round *(rnd)*.

Continue working slip stitches *(sl sts)* in both loops *(lps)* of each half double crochet *(hdc)* around.

Remove first color beginning-of-round *(beg-of-rnd)* stitch marker. (84 slip stitches {sl sts})

Round (rnd) 2: Remembering to make loose chains *(chs)* throughout, make 5 chains *(chs)*.

Place first color stitch marker in front and back loop *(lp)* of 3rd chain *(ch)* made to mark beginning *(beg)* of round *(rnd)*.

Working in both loops *(lps)* of slip stitches *(sl sts)* around,

skip *(sk)* first 2 slip stitches *(sl sts)*.

Double crochet *(dc)* in next slip stitch *(sl st)*.

*Chain *(ch)* 2.

Skip *(sk)* next 2 slip stitches *(sl sts)*.

Double crochet *(dc)* in next slip stitch *(sl st)*.

Repeat *(rep)* from * around to last 2 slip stitches *(sl sts)*.

Chain *(ch)* 2.

Skip *(sk)* last 2 slip stitches *(sl sts)*.

Slip stitch *(sl st)* in front and back loop *(lp)* of marked 3rd chain *(ch)* of beginning *(beg)* chain-5 *(ch-5)* to join round *(rnd)*.

(28 double crochet {dc}, 28 chain-2 spaces {ch-2 sps})

Round (rnd) 3: Make 5 chains *(chs)*.

Move first color stitch marker to front and back loop *(lp)* of 3rd chain *(ch)* made to mark beginning *(beg)* of round *(rnd)*.

Skip *(sk)* chain-2 *(ch-2)* space *(sp)*.

Double crochet *(dc)* in next double crochet *(dc)*.

*Chain *(ch)* 2.

Skip *(sk)* next chain-2 *(ch-2)* space *(sp)*.

Double crochet *(dc)* in next double crochet *(dc)*.

Repeat *(rep)* from * around to last chain-2 *(ch-2)* space *(sp)*.

Chain *(ch)* 2.

Slip stitch *(sl st)* in front and back loop *(lp)* of marked 3rd chain *(ch)* of beginning *(beg)* chain-5 *(ch-5)* to join the round *(rnd)*.

(28 double crochet {dc}, 28 chain-2 spaces {ch-2 sps})

Repeat *(rep)* round *(rnd)* 3 until Outer Bag measures about ¼ inch less than Bag Liner.

Next round (rnd): Chain *(ch)* 1 *(see Pattern Notes)*.

boldface Chain *(ch)*

Single crochet *(sc)* in same chain *(ch)* where join was made.

Move first color stitch marker to stitch *(st)* just made to mark beginning *(beg)* of round *(rnd)*.

*2 single crochet *(sc)* in first chain-2 space *(ch-2 sp)*.

Single crochet *(sc)* in next double crochet *(dc)*.

Window Panes Bag

Repeat (rep) from * around to last chain-2 space (ch-2 sp).

2 single crochet (sc) in last chain-2 space (ch-2 sp).

Drop loop (lp) from hook.

Place a first color stitch marker in dropped loop (lp) to keep it from unraveling. Do not cut yarn.

Finishing

Flatten bag on a table and check to see that the Outer Bag and Bag Liner are the same length. If needed, remove or add a round (rnd) or 2 of single crochet (sc) on the liner to make both pieces the same length.

When Liner and Outer bag are the same length, join the last round (rnd) on the Liner with **invisible join (inv join)** (see page 46) and fasten off.

Remove any 2nd color stitch markers still in Liner.

Flatten bag on table again and adjust so the Outer bag stitches (sts) are straight.

Edging

Round (rnd) 1 (right side {RS}): Remove first color stitch marker from dropped bag loop (lp), then place loop (lp) on hook.

Holding last round (rnd) of both pieces together (tog) and working stitches (sts) through both layers as if they are one,

single crochet (sc) in the marked beginning (beg) of round (rnd) stitch (st).

Move marker to stitch (st) just made.

Continuing to work through both layers,

single crochet (sc) in each remaining (rem) stitch (st) around.

(84 single crochet {sc})

Round (rnd) 2: Single crochet (sc) in each stitch (st) around. *(84 single crochet {sc})*

Round (rnd) 3: Repeat (rep) round (rnd) 2.

Round (rnd) 4: Slip stitch (sl st) in both loops (lps) of each stitch (st) around.

Join round (rnd) with invisible join (inv join) and fasten off.

(84 slip stitches {sl sts})

Remove any remaining (rem) stitch markers from project.

Weave in all yarn ends.

Strap Loop (Lp)
Make 4.

Row 1: With blue, make 7 chains (chs).

Turn to work back across foundation chain (ch).

Skip (sk) first chain (ch) closest to hook.

Single crochet (sc) in back bar of next chain (ch).

Window Panes Bag

Single crochet (sc) in back bar of each remaining (rem) chain (ch) across.

Turn work. (6 single crochet {sc})

Row 2: Chain (ch) 1.

Single crochet (sc) in first stitch (st) and in each stitch (st) across.

Turn work. (6 single crochet {sc})

Repeat (rep) row 2 until strap is 3 inches long, measuring from foundation chain (ch) to last row.

Fasten off at end of last row leaving a 15-inch tail for sewing.

Optional: If you would like to strengthen the Strap Loops (Lps), cut 4 12-inch strands of blue, starting at foundation chain (ch), weave 1 strand up along edge of each strap, going across top row, then down along 2nd edge back to foundation chain (ch). Pull strand taut while keeping strap flat, then weave in ends.

Finishing 4 Strap Loops (Lps)

Turn bag so Liner is on outside of bag, place bag on table then flatten sides. Place a stitch marker on last Liner round (rnd) about 2½ inches in from each side on both front and back of bag to mark Strap Loop (Lp) placement.

For Each Strap

Weave in beginning (beg) strand.

Fold strap in half so foundation chain (ch) is touching last row.

With tapestry needle and 15-inch ending yarn tail,

whipstitch (see page 19) foundation chain (ch) and last row together (tog) forming a loop (lp).

Once all 4 loops (lps) are finished, sew the whipstitched seam to last Liner round (rnd) using stitch markers for placement guide.

Weave in any remaining (rem) yarn ends.

Rope Tie

Cut 2 strands of white 5½ yards long.

Hold strands together (tog), fold in half making 4 ends.

Tie the 4 ends together (tog) in a knot.

Place knotted end onto a stationary object the diameter of a pencil, a 2nd person holding both ends of a pencil works well if no stationary object is available.

Put looped end on finger.

Pull strands taut.

Twist strands 200 times.

Put 1 finger in center of rope then fold rope in half allowing the 2 sides of the rope to twist together (tog) naturally.

Being careful to keep rope twisted, weave rope through Strap Loop (Lp) openings starting on center front of bag.

Make sure rope goes all the way around outer edge of bag then tie rope ends together (tog) in overhand knot so that knot hangs down 1–2 inches on front of bag.

Cut the rope ends open about 3 inches from the knot then unravel ends forming tassel.

Trim tassel to desired length.

Repeat (rep) Rope Tie directions for 2nd rope, weaving 2nd rope through Strap Loop (Lp) openings starting at center back.

Bottom Pad (Optional)
Make 2.

Work Bottom of Bag rounds (rnds) 1–7.

After last stitch (st) is complete, join last round (rnd) with invisible join (inv join).

Weave in beginning (beg) yarn end.

Cut a piece of plastic canvas using 1 Bottom Pad for a template.

Cut a matching strand of yarn 40 inches long.

Hold both pads together (tog) with wrong sides (WS) together (tog).

With tapestry needle and yarn strand,

sew the 2 Bottoms together (tog) using **running stitches** (see illustration) leaving a large enough opening to slide plastic canvas piece inside.

Running Stitch

Place plastic canvas between the 2 pads then finish sewing the 2 pads together (tog) encasing plastic inside.

Place pad in bottom of bag. ●

STITCH GUIDE

Need help? ▶ StitchGuide.com • ILLUSTRATED GUIDES • HOW-TO VIDEOS

STITCH ABBREVIATIONS

beg	begin/begins/beginning
bpdc	back post double crochet
bpsc	back post single crochet
bptr	back post treble crochet
CC	contrasting color
ch(s)	chain(s)
ch-	refers to chain or space previously made (i.e., ch-1 space)
ch sp(s)	chain space(s)
cl(s)	cluster(s)
cm	centimeter(s)
dc	double crochet (singular/plural)
dc dec	double crochet 2 or more stitches together, as indicated
dec	decrease/decreases/decreasing
dtr	double treble crochet
ext	extended
fpdc	front post double crochet
fpsc	front post single crochet
fptr	front post treble crochet
g	gram(s)
hdc	half double crochet
hdc dec	half double crochet 2 or more stitches together, as indicated
inc	increase/increases/increasing
lp(s)	loop(s)
MC	main color
mm	millimeter(s)
oz	ounce(s)
pc	popcorn(s)
rem	remain/remains/remaining
rep(s)	repeat(s)
rnd(s)	round(s)
RS	right side(s)
sc	single crochet (singular/plural)
sc dec	single crochet 2 or more stitches together, as indicated
sk	skip/skipped/skipping
sl st(s)	slip stitch(es)
sp(s)	space(s)/spaced
st(s)	stitch(es)
tog	together
tr	treble crochet
trtr	triple treble
WS	wrong side(s)
yd(s)	yard(s)
yo	yarn over

YARN CONVERSION

OUNCES TO GRAMS	GRAMS TO OUNCES
1 — 28.4	25 — 7/8
2 — 56.7	40 — 1 2/3
3 — 85.0	50 — 1 3/4
4 — 113.4	100 — 3 1/2

UNITED STATES		UNITED KINGDOM
sl st (slip stitch)	=	sc (single crochet)
sc (single crochet)	=	dc (double crochet)
hdc (half double crochet)	=	htr (half treble crochet)
dc (double crochet)	=	tr (treble crochet)
tr (treble crochet)	=	dtr (double treble crochet)
dtr (double treble crochet)	=	ttr (triple treble crochet)
skip	=	miss

Single crochet decrease (sc dec): (Insert hook, yo, draw lp through) in each of the sts indicated, yo, draw through all lps on hook.

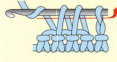

Example of 2-sc dec

Half double crochet decrease (hdc dec): (Yo, insert hook, yo, draw lp through) in each of the sts indicated, yo, draw through all lps on hook.

Example of 2-hdc dec

Reverse single crochet (reverse sc): Ch 1, sk first st, working from left to right, insert hook in next st from front to back, draw up lp on hook, yo and draw through both lps on hook.

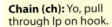

Chain (ch): Yo, pull through lp on hook.

Single crochet (sc): Insert hook in st, yo, pull through st, yo, pull through both lps on hook.

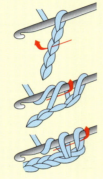

Double crochet (dc): Yo, insert hook in st, yo, pull through st, [yo, pull through 2 lps] twice.

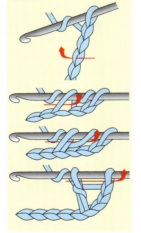

Double crochet decrease (dc dec): (Yo, insert hook, yo, draw lp through, yo, draw through 2 lps on hook) in each of the sts indicated, yo, draw through all lps on hook.

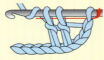

Example of 2-dc dec

Front loop (front lp): Back loop (back lp):

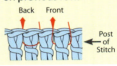

Front Loop   Back Loop

Front post stitch (fp): Back post stitch (bp): When working post st, insert hook from right to left around post of st on previous row.

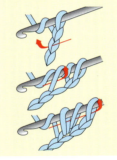

Back   Front   ← Post of Stitch

Half double crochet (hdc): Yo, insert hook in st, yo, pull through st, yo, pull through all 3 lps on hook.

Double treble crochet (dtr): Yo 3 times, insert hook in st, yo, pull through st, [yo, pull through 2 lps] 4 times.

Treble crochet decrease (tr dec): Holding back last lp of each st, tr in each of the sts indicated, yo, pull all lps on hook.

Example of 2-tr dec

Slip stitch (sl st): Insert hook in st, pull through both lps on hook.

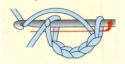

Chain color change (ch color change): Yo with new color, draw through last lp on hook.

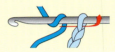

Double crochet color change (dc color change): Drop first color, yo with new color, draw through last 2 lps of st.

Treble crochet (tr): Yo twice, insert hook in st, yo, pull through st, [yo, pull through 2 lps] 3 times.

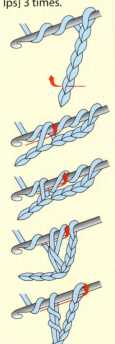

Metric Conversion Charts

METRIC CONVERSIONS

yards	x	.9144	=	meters (m)
yards	x	91.44	=	centimeters (cm)
inches	x	2.54	=	centimeters (cm)
inches	x	25.40	=	millimeters (mm)
inches	x	.0254	=	meters (m)
centimeters	x	.3937	=	inches
meters	x	1.0936	=	yards

INCHES INTO MILLIMETERS & CENTIMETERS (Rounded off slightly)

inches	mm	cm	inches	cm	inches	cm	inches	cm
1/8	3	0.3	5	12.5	21	53.5	38	96.5
1/4	6	0.6	5 1/2	14	22	56	39	99
3/8	10	1	6	15	23	58.5	40	101.5
1/2	13	1.3	7	18	24	61	41	104
5/8	15	1.5	8	20.5	25	63.5	42	106.5
3/4	20	2	9	23	26	66	43	109
7/8	22	2.2	10	25.5	27	68.5	44	112
1	25	2.5	11	28	28	71	45	114.5
1 1/4	32	3.2	12	30.5	29	73.5	46	117
1 1/2	38	3.8	13	33	30	76	47	119.5
1 3/4	45	4.5	14	35.5	31	79	48	122
2	50	5	15	38	32	81.5	49	124.5
2 1/2	65	6.5	16	40.5	33	84	50	127
3	75	7.5	17	43	34	86.5		
3 1/2	90	9	18	46	35	89		
4	100	10	19	48.5	36	91.5		
4 1/2	115	11.5	20	51	37	94		

KNITTING NEEDLES CONVERSION CHART

Canada/U.S.	0	1	2	3	4	5	6	7	8	9	10	10½	11	13	15
Metric (mm)	2	2¼	2¾	3¼	3½	3¾	4	4½	5	5½	6	6½	8	9	10

CROCHET HOOKS CONVERSION CHART

Canada/U.S.	1/B	2/C	3/D	4/E	5/F	6/G	7	8/H	9/I	10/J	10½/K	N
Metric (mm)	2.25	2.75	3.25	3.5	3.75	4	4.5	5	5.5	6	6.5	9.0

Notes: